JACK NICHOLSON

Calum Cumming

chipmunkapublishing
the mental health publisher

Calum Cumming

All rights reserved, no part of this publication may be reproduced by any means, electronic, mechanical photocopying, documentary, film or in any other format without prior written permission of the publisher.

>Published by
>Chipmunkapublishing
>United Kingdom

http://www.chipmunkapublishing.com

Copyright © Calum Cumming 2017

ISBN   978-1-78382-338-3

Because of the dynamic nature of the Internet, any web addresses or links contained in this book may have changed since publication and may no longer be valid. The views expressed in this work are solely those of the author and do not necessarily reflect the views of the publisher, and the publisher hereby disclaims any responsibility for them.

ABOUT THE AUTHOR

Calum Cumming is fifty-one. He was born in Scotland and raised in the northeast and northwest islands. He is a time-served engineer and a classics graduate from Glasgow. He is educated in the university of life as well as formally. His parents divorced when he was three, and he was raised by his mother, Betsy Caird. His Father died in 1996 in the Outer Hebrides from smoking and drinking, a metaphor for Scotland. For this year, the country has the chance of independence, where the people can finally discard the thistles that plague their souls.

Calum Cumming

CHAPTER ONE

A rain dance is a dancing ceremony performed by some Native American tribes asking their spirits or Gods to send rain. It is more common among Southwest Native Americans who live in drier regions.

The rain dance normally takes place during the spring planting season and the summer months before crops are harvested. The dance asks the Gods or spirits to send the appropriate amount of rain at the correct time to assure a plentiful crop.

Standing.
Waiting to board a flight with my wife Lou.
"I phoned him Lou I got through"
"What did he say," Said Lou; "I spoke to Norman . . . my father . . . I mean I spoke to him."
My first trip to America-The METAGAMA of the Celts from Lewis to North America-Lou read the book in Aberdeen (Scotland). The Celtic Diaspora.

"He said, Jim," if you have to go you have to go. America Jim my jumbled up roots. Your black silk cheater is woven "SCORPIO" in gold silk writing. I mean me standing here behind her I completely love Lou my young wife.

They both have spinal injuries-Lou's is worse than his-car accident in Minnesota when she was a teenager-Jim the building industry he fell off a scaffold.

They share that secret in common-it's how they got talking in that flat up in that party in 36 Otago street in Glasgow some three years ago now. Its okay now-they massage one another.

Accident; Lou has two fused vertebrae and he has a partial right fracture of the eighth vertebrae. Never healed.

It was a Friday night when Jim met Lou in Glasgow, for Friday's child was always a hard worker—it was May, mellow May and Jim's birthday. The party was thrown to commemorate a very special friend of Lou's-Prince Mustafa El Gamal-Doctor of Philosophy and Moroccan political prisoner from Marrakech. He had got his doctorate in Glasgow and now he was in a Paris jail for political subversion. Lou later told Jim that Mustafa was a Gemini tiger-the twin star-almost me, he used to tell a lot of jokes and his party piece was What does Saddam Hussein and Larry Grayson got in common? Saddam no like Bush. One Lou told me and once when he was sharing a flat with Lou he had this Lebanese girlfriend Carla from the west bank of Lebanon. He used to declare with a flourish, "Carla easy Carla good".

Lou stood in line and waited with her husband. Waiting to board this flight from Abbots inch airport in Glasgow to Chicago O' Hare. She looked over her shoulder at Jim he looked haunted somehow. He had said there is an antrin couth borealis light in the North East.

It was hardly she hollered "Jim I'm starving",
"I be quiet now bon dakor we will soon be aboard".

JACK NICHOLSON

Soon they were moving to passport control and Lou noticed a man with a caste; arm in a navy blue sling- he stared at Her womanly body stubbornly as he caught her silent glance.

She has been in the USA. What's changed she wondered?
Lou's a graduate now-MA Humanities and Jim had a degree in Civil Engineering.
They will stay.
Ned and Judith and her twin sister Betsy Joe would be waiting for them in Portland to drive the 120 miles on i5 to Swiss cottage in Eugene. Lou's mother is Swiss by descent and her father Scots-a MACLEOD.

They were going to buy a car and drive down to California and then on to Mexico. Lou's brother Jimmy lived in Los Angeles where he was a junior oil executive with Unocal. Lou was raised in Ventura County.

They were traveling economy class and Jim was seated in front of Lou in the center aisle. She felt sad that She was apart from her husband and when the plane took off she felt like crying but the woman next to her gave her a butterscotch sweetie for her ears. Lou suddenly thought about how Jim had said She had a scabby monkey ear-her car accident-little lugs; Jim's pet name for her was capuche-the little cheeky 68' monkey. Damned cheek-Lou is 5' 9".

Well pretty soon they were on their way with drinks and quickly the quaint little airline meals came their way. It was chicken satay with sticky rice one of Lou's favorites. Lou will definitely fly Continental again she thought.

Lou was so excited to be returning to America, the fun park of the USA. After dinner and drinks the airline movie came on it was Frankie and Mannienie with Al Pacino and Michelle Pfeifer, nothing could go wrong now she thought.

Jim was seated next to this big bear of a Glaswegian called Ronnie. He was flying on to Miami-they were going to Portland in Oregon. Lou kept noticing that little man with the caste and the sling. He was situated over the wing in a window seat. Maybe it was an omen. Lou fired Jim up a smoke and handed him the pack of Regals-they had bought a carton at duty free together with a 40 ounce of Chivas Regal for Ned and Judith.

Lou settled into the long flight everything was stowed and waiting to go.

Ten alert hours later they were at Chicago O' Hare and disembarking. Jim said goodbye to Ronnie and went to be with his wife Lou. He noticed two guys at the stern of the plane at the cargo bay sitting in a Willies Jeep; one of them had his feet cock sure perched on the steering wheel. He was wearing cowboy boots. He had on mirror shades and a white fair-isle pullover. He was wearing a black aviatrix leather jacket. He stared at Jim. He looked at him intently and he looked like that little Irish American actor guy Sean Penn. Welcome to America-the wedding design.

Lou was so excited to be back home. The vast airport concourse extended to the concrete water towers in the infinity. Pretty soon they were on the bus traveling to the terminal building with all the other passengers waiting to be tracked through customs and immigration. Lou held Jim's hand tenderly and nuzzled into his Taurean neck. C'mon feel the noise!

All too soon they were at immigration and Jim came through the green lane with Lou. Jim told her that most of the Americans coming through customs had been based at the Holy loch-the submarine base. Jim's dad Norman had been a submariner in the war and he had two tattoos. One was a navy blue seaman on his hairy forearm and it read "Scotland forever" and the other was a red and black hope and anchor on his upper right arm. Lou had a tattoo on her right foreleg-it is a green serpent entwined round a black commando dagger and she had it done in sorority up in Tacoma Bay. She was very proud of it. She wanted Jim to get a tattoo. That would make her very happy if he got her names tattooed on his arm.

Jim spoke to the immigration officer and the officer said he was right to come through the green lane with his wife and beat the people standing in line.

"Lou"

"C'mon my little lima bean I'll treat you to a Chicago hot dog and a bottle of Bud."

The first thing that struck Jim about America was the slick colors-all aluminum and red white and blue stripes. That and how fresh young and friendly everyone was. There was real bustle of many people and cultures coming and going. The melting pot of the USA.

Lou walked ahead and Jim stared at her sexy bum in her black Armani's the ones he had got her for her birthday. Lou's black red hair hung in serpents on her back-her little hunch would need massaging tonight Jim thought.

They made love most nights. Jim hoped her parent's would understand when they slip off early. Pretty soon they were at the café and ordering their hot dogs. Jim had green relish with his. It tasted wonderful. It is not the only sausage Lou is getting today he chuckled to his self. Lou said-"what are you laughing at Jim! What makes you laugh is seeing me put this big sausage in my mouth". He burst out laughing and had a gulp of Bud. He could have devoured the little sugar muffin.
Their flight was in two hours and they went to check in for the flight. They were flying American Airlines.

Jim sparked Lou up with a Galois-she had started smoking them in Aberdeen. She gave him a drag and he started to chase her through the terminal building towards the American Airlines check in. He was desperate for a kiss. Lou is a fast runner and when he caught up with the little pussycat he was panting.

Lou said, "I love you Jim you goofball." And she took a drag on the Galois and roached it on the concrete of the terminal. Suddenly they were in an embrace and Jim slipped my hand inside Lou's black windcheater. Her nipples were like stogies.

"You know Jim I am so ashamed of my roots-low born people," said Lou. Jim suddenly thought it was over three years since Lou had seen her family. He replied panting, "We are all aristocrats Lou-it is just that you were born an incandescent beauty; a Madonna that came in from the country." "It's funny Jim I feel like about turning and taking the first plane back to Glasgow" said Lou. Jim replied, "Lets see how I get on with Ned and Judith Lou-you is an independent spirit, now, they weren't happy when we got married. Lou-part of the highborn middle class Lewis men-bright eyes, good teeth strong and tall-the Macleods." "I know Jim but the middle classes of Aberdeen take control while the rest well . . . they are totally out of control." Said Lou. "Oh baby Lou I want to be with you that's all that matters- we are family _now_." Said Jim. "I just . . . Jim . . . lets go and check in". "Lou I am not American and I don't go around saying I love you to everyone I meet . . . but I do love you and that is all to me, your love". "What's not to love Jim I sacrificed a lot for you and now I want you to hold me forever".

They broke apart and did their job-produced their tickets and Lou moved away from Jim. Jim then moved a little closer to Lou and put his arm around her. The onrushing crush stared at the glamorous young couple-a tousled twosome.

Soon after checking in they were in the departure lounge. Lou was still a little upset and her husband did his best to cheer her up. "It's funny Lou how you were born in the year of the cat and I was born in the year of the tiger" both primates replied Lou confidently-except I'm a sex kitten. She was a little bored now and had her compact out attending to a little spot on her cheek. Lou had Jim in her Venus fly trap. "I mean Lou I am 28 and you are 22 there is six

years between us." Said Jim. Lou merely pulled up her jean bottoms above her calf and her serpent tattoo and replied, "Six Jim".
Jim suddenly felt crestfallen and resumed looking at the airplanes taking off and landing. Soon Lou had put her compact away and gave Jim a kiss on the cheek showing her affection for him.

Pretty soon they were embarking-it was getting dark it was nearly six thirty. Once they were seated Lou said, "look at the people-Jim-where do they all belong, these are all Portland people-mostly men wearing brown or beige. "Jim and Lou were sitting over the left wing and Jim suddenly looked to his right and saw the little man with the caste and the sling. He was flying on to Portland in Oregon.

"I feel drained Lou." Said Jim. He was sitting in the window seat and they were an hour into their short haul flight. Lou had been reading her novel she had her black horn rimmed glasses on-IT was Grey Granite by Lewis Grassic Gibbon-she was obsessed with Aberdeen Jim thought it was where He was brought up. The thought lifted Jim that Lou carried a torch for him always. Lou thoughtfully asked the stewardess for a pillow for his head. Pretty quickly they were chatting, Lou said, "Its my husbands first trip to the USA he's from Scotland."

They were flying low-the whole way. Jim saw all these nameless towns and He could make out people down below. It was beautiful-all these different communities and all these different peoples-Jim felt like a god flying low across America.

Jim didn't speak to Lou; she had her nose stuck in

her book. As she went backwards Jim flew towards-over the nests-people just going about their lives-it fascinated him.

All too soon they were at Portland PDX and the plane made to land. Lou put her book away-God Aberdeen is a gray dreich place she thought although it is true to say that the granite has a sparkling ethereal beauty. I don't suppose Lou will ever be back there again, (Jim's father lived in Harris in the Outer Hebrides now, and Jim didn't have any friends in Aberdeen). Jim said, "look Lou it's real misty outside it is going to be a tough landing". Jim had his nose stuck to the window and were both like rabbits caught in the headlights. The announcement came on to buckle up and extinguish cigarettes. They made their descent through the mist and cloud. Lou suddenly thought this is Jesus (my JIM) making his way down to earth to do some good and make a positive difference to America-She was so proud of her husband. He was her hero. The feeling just gets stronger with every passing moment and day.

Find me in the sunshine Jim. I watched as the nebulous swirl flew past and suddenly held Jim's hand. Suddenly we were down and in Portland. The airbrakes took hold and we snaked and slithered along the runway. Rain town this is Portland okay. Suddenly they were taxing towards the concourse where Ned Judith and Betsy Joe my twin sister would be waiting. Jim was glad to be getting off the plane-he was jetlagged and this was his first long haul flight since he had been a child returning from the Sudan. Jim suddenly told Lou, "When I was a kid returning from the Sudan I pissed on the arm of Peter Scott the naturalist-at least so my Mom told me." You cheeky little otter Jim," Said Lou who stole a kiss.

Soon they were inside the terminal and right enough Lou's family was not waiting for them. They went to the carousel and got their bags. Jim went to use the toilet while Lou waited for him outside it was pitch black outside.

The water came out the hot from the cold and I could not turn on the faucet. I reckoned it was just a question of different systematic beliefs that is all-a hitch. Finally Jim figured it out his civils brain kicked in. He went back outside and found Lou reunited with her family. Jim had met Ned in Glasgow but this was the first time as a couple they had met Judith and Betsy Joe. Ned was wearing a Boston Celts tracksuit and white Merrell trainers. Ned shook Jim's hand warmly and he looked at him with sensitive blue eyes. Jim turned to Judith She wore glasses and declared, "Well how are you doing Jim" "I'm great Judith," said Jim and he kissed and embraced her-the old world meets the new. Judith suddenly thought if I could turn back the hands of time I would be yours and yours alone young Jim.

Betsy Joe was a bit overweight and Lou reckoned she had been left up on the mantelpiece. Lou had told Jim her knowledge of Hollywood was second to none and her favorite actor was Burl Ives- "concentrate but you cant because your brains all soaked with liquor" (Cat On a Hot Tin Roof). They shook hands and Jim gave her a peck.

Ned was a basketball coach retired and he had been a high school teacher in Southern Ca. Jim and Ned shared a love of golf. Pretty soon they would be on the fairways and at the practice range. Jim had recently had an operation on his right hand that was bandaged up. Jim asked Ned. "What is the matter with your hand?" "Goddamn monkey burn-polyps I wasn't made for sunny weather".

Lou talked with her Mom and her sister as Jim and Ned walked ahead pushing the carousel towards the car that was waiting outside. Pretty soon they were on the freeway making for Eugene-the car was a Nissan Primera and Jim thought he liked Japanese cars. He rode up front with Ned. Jim was like the man with the child in his eyes. This was a brand new culture-Everything was a slick and red tailgates on the freeway.

Calum Cumming

CHAPTER TWO

They both woke late they were naked in the double bed. Jim kissed Lou's vagina, as usual-it was all fishy from last night's sex.

Jim heard Ned and Judith in the kitchen and Jim wondered where BJ was. He asked Lou-she said "BJ will be in her bedroom she doesn't get out of there too often Jim".

It made him wonder-Lou had told Jim in Scotland that BJ had Schizoid affective psychosis and was on Lithium carbonate. Jim suddenly thought of all the letters that BJ had written to Lou in Glasgow-they all had a fine tremor in the writing-the side effects of Lithium.

"I'm going for a shower Jim," said Lou and she was out the door in her dressing gown. Jim drew the curtains on the bedroom window and looked out-it was light now.

The timber built house looked out on to pine trees. They were in Timberline drive. Jim had noticed last night that the blue and white house was called Swiss cottage. There was a Toyota helix pick up sitting in the drive with a set of golf clubs in the back-Ned must have been playing golf Jim thought. He looked upwards and around the street, it was deserted. The pavement was made of concrete and he noticed that the curbs were cast in one-no curb race. Everything was intact and clean.

It was mild as Jim poked his head out of the window-clean and mild-that is what money bought you Jim thought-mild seven cigars. He then looked left into the small exclusive estate there was a bike lying discarded outside one of the houses just laying there. Judith and Ned had the corner site. He noticed all the mailboxes with their red arms pointing up into the wispy blue sky-here you got your mail picked up as well as delivered. He suddenly thought of Charles Bukowski and the novel office. Jim had given a copy to Mustafa in Otago Street. Jim reflected on him ruefully for a few seconds. The material distress of Europe and the USA seemed a long way away. He turned away from the window and he looked around the bedroom. On the wall was a small mirror with Johnny Walker whisky written on it. It was a parody of Scotland and he chuckled to myself Judith was not without a sense of humor Jim thought.

Everything was in reverse he thought and to put the light on you pushed the switch up. Why can't just everything be the same he thought-where was 00 gauge now! It was understandable that America was in some fundamental sense a protest to king George.The Boston tea party and all that. White Protestants. He went to get dressed Jim would have a shower later and wash off the smell of Lou's cunt. For now he was content to let it linger.

Jim went through to the kitchen-there was the smell of coffee. Judith asked him to sit at the breakfast table and poured Jim a cup of Folgers Blue affricated. He enjoyed it with white sugar and half and half. It would soon be Christmas and Jim's cup was half full. Before Judith retired she had been a radiographer-she took x-rays. Jim suddenly thought of the little man in his caste on the plane and tried to put it from his mind.

Judith said to Jim "I spent a year in Oxford before I met Ned Jim I liked it in your old world". Judith was wearing gray slacks and a blue rayon sweater, she came and sat down beside him and looked at Jim with warm brown eyes from behind bifocals. Her gray blonde hair was done up in tresses. "I don't know what we would have done without your Brit rail Jim". He suddenly blurted out, "I think you have more Gas in America Judith". Judith started laughing for Jim was yet to enter the commercial world of American TV where there was a cure for every kind of Gas imaginable. Ned came into the kitchen he was wearing a timberland golf cheater. Judith said, "Jim thinks we have more gas in America" and Ned started laughing. Ned came and sat down and Jude fixed him some coffee,he took it black with sugar. It was the best coffee Jim had ever tasted.

Quickly BJ came into the kitchen-she was dressed and Jim rose to give up his seat for her but she said "No Jim". He couldn't quite believe she was Lou's twin-she was blonde, with corn blue eyes and looked a little like the Pillsbury dough boy.

BJ had been a cheerleader in high school before she became unwell at sixteen-she hadn't been able to graduate from high school because of her Bi-polar.

BJ was excited it seemed, Jim could see that Ned was protective of her-
, it didn't even occur to him whether she was still a virgin or not. BJ went to get her medication in the cupboard. Jim would get used to that door opening and shutting over the next month. BJ told Jim quickly after she had taken her tablets that she had a job interview with the American Red Cross today in Eugene. "It's a voluntary administrative post Jim but I hope it will lead to something better". Ned looked at his daughter tenderly.

Suddenly BJ looked out into the back garden and saw a gray squirrel doing a crazy spiral up a pine tree then back down. They all crammed to look and burst out laughing. "It must be altitude sickness," said Ned.

The shower room was downstairs next to the Den and BJ's bedroom. Lou had finished showering and BJ had lent Lou her vosene shampoo. Lou now buttered up her body with some Oil of Olay. She took care with her hands and particularly the skin graft on her left pinkie. It was a reminder of Lou's car accident in Minnesota when she had gone through the windshield driven by Deke. That drunken fool Lou thought. She quickly looked in the mirror and noticed the scar on her left temple-the deep weal was another reminder of Deke. She was lucky not to lose an eye. Jim had told her the scar gave her character-there was someone looking out for you that night Lou said Jim.

Lou dried her hair in a tic with BJs' red Revlon hair drier and tried to forget about her past in America-this was a new start for Jim and Lou. Looking into the beginning of her existence.

Blue green eyes; black from a distance. She was married now to the reed of my Life magazine. A story about the cast system in Hollywood-a system so ugly and pernicious that it was beyond comprehension. Yet in this system the name COMING was placed first. And that is where Jim had always tried to come-FIRST. On the Arab prayer day of Friday at eight minutes to midday. My husband would maybe eventually unite the Arab world with Hollywood's help.

Lou went upstairs and put clothes on, she fixed her hair in a bun. Lou heard the sound of family laughter from the kitchen and it made her happy that Jim was getting on with her loving inner family.

Lou sat down on the bed and looked at her painted purple toenails. She gave them a little wiggle like a piggy. Jim had not had a shower-ugh! He is so venal. Lou remembered when they got married Stuart (another bovine personality) got them a hen salmon as a wedding present. Jim merely put it out the back window cill for later consumption. They had the fish the next day, the hen was crammed full of roe. Now I wouldn't say Jim was dirty but he could shower a bit more often I thought-filthy European poets.

Lou put yellow socks on and her black Merrell trainers. Jack Macleod was the richest old hippy in Oregon. He had made his money in microbrewery pubs and picture houses. Cousin Jack was 76 now and looked about 50. He colored his hair but he looked young for his age. Lou giggled when she thought of him-he was a very amusing man. Cousin Jack swore you were only as old as the woman you felt. Lou had consumed a few pints of excellent ale with Cousin Jack.

Jim would be meeting cousin Jack in due course. . .

The next couple of days passed in domestic harmony. Jim opened a bank account with the Wells Fargo bank and deposited his $8,000. Pretty soon Jim and Lou decided they would have to buy a car. They both scoured the Eugene paper and looked in the Safeway's ads for a car. They circled a few likely contenders and Ned took them to see the motors. After having seen a couple of bangers Jim phoned and then got the bus to see an old guy on his own. The car was silver Toyota Corolla-it was for sale for $800 with two spare tires. Jim really hit it off with the old man and he asked Jim in for a coffee after he had test driven the car. They sat in the old man's front room drinking coffee. The man's name was Bob Ellingham. Jim noticed the man had several photos of himself in military uniform. Jim said-"Did you serve in the forces Bob?"

"Sure did said Bob" with an air of resignation; "I was in the Marine Corp in Korea". Bob said-"I met quite a few Scots Guards." Jim chuckled. He could tell that Bob was a really decent man and that he didn't really want to sell the car but somehow Jim thought it would make him happy if it went to a good home. "She likes to sit at 55mph and won't give you any trouble Jim".

The deal was done and Jim paid cash in $20 bills, his first American car, he was delighted. Bob came out the front with him and shook his hand. He wished Jim good luck, as he would never see Jim again. Jim thanked Bob for such a piece of fortune running into an honest Korean Vet.

Jim took off it was a new life all right. He drove through the concrete streets and pretty soon realized the way home to Swiss Cottage. When he got in Judith was making pancakes and she was delighted that Jim had bought a car. She said. "Well how do you do Mr. Cumming man". Jim asked Jude where Lou was, "She's in the shower Jim she was out cycling this afternoon on the white bike". Jim skipped down the stairs and knocked on the shower room door-He said, "Can I come in Lou I got a car." Lou let him in and he took her naked body in his arms-"I got a car Lou"-"OH Jim," said Lou "We're halfway there then." Jim locked the door and had an erection coming on. They kissed wildly and Jim bent down on his legs and pushed Lou roughly against the shower room wall. He spread her legs tenderly and gorged on her vagina. She was warming moist and musky. Her clitoris was stiff and erect and Jim licked her clitoris gently. He tenderly withdrew the hood with his fingers and licked and kissed the glans of her little penis.

Lou had a petit mort and collapsed against the wall. Jim stood up and pulled his trousers and pants down. Lou shouted, "Take me Jim." Lou took the shaft of his penis and gently entered her moist and musky vagina. His erection was enormous. Lou hooked her legs up and Jim held her legs. He started pumping his shaft rhythmically his penis was so fat he could feel Lou's coil at the tip of his fat cock. Suddenly Jim felt a smell of must sweep up from Lou's vaginal glands-it only served to make him more excited. Lou's nipples were huge and engorged with blood.

Suddenly there was a knock at the door it was BJ she needed the toilet. She must have heard Lou's moans from the bedroom next door. Jim's hard on wilted like a lopped daisy at the thought of BJ at the door. Meanwhile the silver Toyota sat silently outside. The air was thick with the smell of Lou's wet cunt. Jim unhooked and quickly pulled up his pants and trousers. Lou quickly got into her robe and flushed the toilet. She pumped some air freshener into the air. Jim unlocked the door and was faced with BJ.

BJ was wearing a floral print frock dress that spread down over her fat body like a teepee. BJ said to Lou, "Huh, what are you doing in the toilet with James." Lou snapped back, "Mind your own fucking business you fat cow." Jim tactfully withdrew himself from the ensuing scene and went upstairs to the kitchen and Judith. He passed the open bedroom door of Ned and Judith's bedroom. (Ned was lying on the bed like a little child watching basketball on the television. Ned was oblivious to Jim,he had on his Boston Celts tracksuit and was in white socks. Jim thought it was the strangest thing in the world to see an old man lying like a street boy on top of the bed in the middle of the day.) James said to Ned I bought a car. Ned replied in his slow east coast Schenectady accent, "That's tremendous Jim."

Jim went into the kitchen and sat down. Jude asked Jim if he wanted some juice,"No I'm good Judith." Jim was pretty hungry from his afternoon's work and

Judith gave him a stack of butterscotch pancakes served with unsalted butter and maple syrup. It sure did help to make up for the disappointment of his union with his wife (he would bash the bishop in the toilet on his own later, mixed sexual thoughts)...

Lou went upstairs got dressed and joined Jim and Judith in the kitchen. "The car looks great Jim," said Lou, "I will phone cousin Jack this afternoon and he will arrange some car insurance then we're set to hit the road in the New Year," said Lou. "You'll like cousin Jack," said Judith.

Jim took Lou for a ride in their new car-they went down to Safe ways; Jim needed shaving foam and Lou was going to buy a bottle of red wine to celebrate.

Jim soon discovered that you are allowed to turn right on a red light in America.

How sensible! No overtaking at intersections the cops will pull you over for that. They soon arrived at the free parking lot of Safeway's and parked up. Lou and Jim held hands as they walked towards the entrance. There was a jakie sitting at the entrance with a cardboard sign saying, "Will work for food and lodgings".

Jesus welcome to America. Operation Desert storm had just ended and Lou and Jim had watched the gruesome images of Kuwait back in Glasgow. Lou gave the man five dollars and said he should definitely get a hot meal for that Lou soon discovered that he was a Vietnam vet. Jim and Lou were meeting cousin Jack in the Vets club tonight and he had set up insurance for the car with Farmers Union mutual insurance coy. It was a present for their wedding.

It was a large 24-hour Safeways. Lou told Jim that all the fruit was waxed to make it more appealing and right enough the lemons shone uniformly under the neon strip light.

They went to get his shaving cream-Lou preferred Jim clean shaven, the stubble made her face nippy when he kissed her, although she did like to see Jim unshaven. She said it made him look sexy.

Jim settled for a can of cinnamon Barbasol,little would he know that can of shaving cream would last him four months of daily shaving and it was thick and creamy; far superior to the British Gillette stuff. They walked past all the shiny happy people towards the drinks aisle. You can only buy beer and wine in Oregon supermarkets, (it's different in California). If you want hard liquor you have to go to the liquor store. How sensible! Lou was 22 only a year older than the legal limit for buying booze. Lou had taken the driving test in UK as her American license had expired. She was a great driver and she could use her UK license as proof of ID now they were in America. She had learned to drive in a Ford Fiesta at the Ashley driving school up in Aberdeen.

"What kind of wine do you want Jim looked at the price of Napa red, $6.48, cheap as chips, and he would soon discover real quality. Jim was beginning to really like America. He said to Lou, "I would like to get some American cigarettes." Lou said, "You ask for a pack Jim they don't work in twenties here they will think you mean twenty packets!" They went to the cigarette Kiosk and Jim asked Lou which packet was Like Regals. Lou said, "Get a pack of Old Gold they are just like Regals, cousin Jack smokes them."

Jim got the smokes and soon he was sitting smoking one. Lou had one and was driving their car with an Old Gold hanging out of her mouth. Old Gold's tasted good-a real deep draw and they lasted almost as long as a Regal. Jim looked at Lou and fell in love with her again.

They went in past Wendy's on the strip and got drive thru cheeseburgers and fries. Just like George Foreman advertised them on the TV. On the way they tail gated behind an old Chevy that was spilling smoke. Jim looked at the telegraph poles carrying all the power cables. It hung sadly like native Cherokees in the late afternoon light. It got dark in the North West pacific suddenly at 5:30 at this time of year. They made it home just as it got dark. Lou looked seraphic in the gloaming as they got out of the car. An angel. Lou took Jim tenderly in her arms and said, "Let's stay Jim".

They ate their cheeseburgers in the Den in front of the TV. The wine was tremendous,mildly alcoholic but not soporific like aphoristic Scottish heavy beer. Lou said, "I got a JF Kennedy half-dollar in the change from Wendy's Jim." BJ came out of her room and Lou showed her the coin. It was a large silver coin with JF Kennedy's head on it. "That's lucky Jim," said BJ and she went back into her darkened cave and her solitary TV.

They watched the Jay Leno show on TV, it was all

LA glitz and glamour and he was interviewing Dennis Rodman the basketball star. Dennis seemed pretty implausible until Jay asked him about his affair with Madonna. "I couldn't possibly comment," he said. Lou said she had read in the National Enquirer at the checkout in Safeway's that Madonna wasn't soul food in bed for him although she wasn't a dead fish either. "Little slipper," shouted Jim.

They went and got ready to meet cousin Jack. Jim had a shave and changed his shirt. He put on his claret denim Levi jacket. The one Lou had bought him in Aberdeen. Lou said she would drive, the Vets club was in McArthur avenue, Downtown. Lou had on her black beret and drove hunched forward with a Galois perched on her bottom lip. They parked up and Jim watched the switch of Lou's derriere as they crossed the avenue towards the Vets club.

They went in and Lou showed her father's membership card and signed Jim in. Lou led Jim into the bar-it was warm and bright with a TV on the basketball above the bar in the corner. Jim looked out the window a snow shower had started biting and infinitely mild. And there was cousin Jack he was wearing the same Levi jacket, as Jim except his one was maroon. C'mon you reds! He was sitting laid back at the bar and he had just finished a large pork chop. Jim gave Jack a bright smile and immediately realized he would love Jack. Lou was suppressing a giggle by sticking her tongue to the inside of the front of her mouth.

Lou looked at Jim then looked at Jack-then burst out laughing. Jack's hair was colored chestnut and was slaistered to his skull-high up on his receding brow was a bruise. Jack stood and gave Lou a bear hug- She could smell Coco Channel on him and the smell of nicotine. Jack introduced himself as "Jack" to Jim and gave him a bone-crushing handshake. Jack said tenderly "What are you both drinking Louise". We'll have cokes replied Lou. Pretty soon the old barman came over like a seal and brought the drinks, (probably he was a SEAL thought Jack). Jack had a vodka martini. "You know why I drink these" said Jack slowly and deliberately to the SEAL, "One of my heroes William Burroughs used to drink these". The Seal replied knowingly as he proffered the change, "Is that how you got the bruise cousin Jack". They all started laughing and Jack said, "The bullet bounced off my pineapple skull!" This place was like the British Legion thought Jim there were military pennants photographs and cap badges all over the walls. Jack asked Lou what was the badge she was wearing on the right hand side of her beret. She replied "courage" it's the COMING family motto". Jim looked at his wife lovingly. A boogie-woogie track suddenly came on in the jukebox in the corner. "Let's go and get a seat courageous Lou," said Jack. They went over and sat in a red veloured open booth by the pool table.

Jim automatically asked cousin Jack what regiment he had been in. Jack replied, "I was in the Air National Guard 1957-62". "You must have done quite a few jumps". "I was mostly on crossing Guard on the Mexican border". "We're going to Mexico Jack," said Lou who had been drinking on her straw of coke. "Well you look after each other in that case "Said Jack seriously. "We're going to Baja" said Jim- "the Sea of Cortez to see the Old Man and The Sea".

"Mexicans are very spiritual peasant people they will be proud to welcome you Jim," said Jack. "Take the border south of San Diego at Mexicale and make for the fishing resort of San Felipe, it's about 150miles south down the Baja" peninsula. Don't stop on the road there's bandits in them there country, but if you break down the white angels will help you. You can either camp on the beach or get a decent motel room." "Jim has a good car Jack she likes to sit at 55mph," said Louise.

That reminds me said Jack, "Here is your car insurance, it is fully comprehensive and will allow both of you to drive in the great mystery of Mexico. You both sign here." Jim and Lou both signed eagerly.

Jack was taken with Jim, JC he thought perhaps he is Coming. Of course both Jack and Jim had rain hot nuts, it was all part of the deal. You fancy a game of pool Jim said cousin Jack. "All right Jack rack them up," said Jim lets shoot pool. Eight ball. Jack suddenly thought what do you do with a boy like this. Lou was looking at the basketball and Jack thought Jim as he looked at her was the luckiest man in the world. Lou suddenly caught Jack's stare and shouted out low and Texan, "Play them balls James beat the fucker". Of course there was a tiny amount of antipathy between Jack and Lou, they were both Texans originally after all.

Jack said maturely "British rules Jim, two shots carry on and last pocket played is the black". Jack has lost weight thought Lou-his ass looks beautiful breaking off left handed in his black armanis. Jack hit the balls with a crack (Jim had lost the toss) and Jack had chalked his cue. The balls went everywhere like Vietnam.

Jim thought deeply and chalked his cue under the ubiquitous strip lighting of the bar. He was left-handed although he wrote with his right hand. He knocked in the green stripe into the bottom left hand pocket-"I'm on stripes Jack," said Jim. The balls were medicinal and spread everywhere. Jim took a wild crack at the stripe red five without chalking his cue. It left Jack on the yellow dot three balls. Jack knocked it in with score, he was a child of the sixties after all. Jack then proceeded to clean up,hit a surgical.

Jack was on the black eight in no time and he knocked it in the pocket. "I'm no match for you cousin Jack," said Jim. "I feel like an absolute beginner," said Jim.

"C'mon get your pool head on," said Jack as he put more quarters into the pool table. Jack racked up and Jim sat beside his wife. Lou laughed and said, "He's not that good Jim he was just showing off. Let me have a game," said Louise. She took off her black beret and her lustrous coiled serpents fell about her shoulders. Lou took the cue and broke off with a hard crack-she was right handed. Two stripes fell in the pockets for the living doll. She then knocked in the green stripe. Jim sat and sucked on his juice. He lit up one of Lou's Galois and took a deep draw. He felt so happy to be with his wife and her cousin Jack. Jim was elated. Lou missed her next shot and came over and took a draw of Jim's cigarette. Jim put his arm around Lou provocatively and drew her waist to his face,he had a semi on. "That's enough of that Jim," said Jack. Jim took the cue and went to take the next shot. Jack had knocked the black on and it was sitting over the middle right hand bag. Something has to give thought Jack. Jim knocked in a stripe then the black went in off-he was jinxed and he said, "Jack have you ever played pro." Jack said, "I'm not going to be at the top much longer three or four years and that will be It." he added, "I don't like the hassle anymore. I'd like to have a good hard four years of pool and then quit the game and get on with life. I prefer women to shooting pool." Lou started laughing ecstatically, "You definitely sure are a card JM," said Lou. "Okay kids," said Jack and he came over and finished his vodka martini. "What do you want to do now said Jack?" Can was a cameo movie house on Main street and Jack had just had it renovated, "It opens next week" said Jack "There's a hundred bucket seats in there. We'll go up to the cine room and watch some movies if you both want to do that," said Jack. Jim said for Lou "We'd love to cousin Jack."

They all made to go,the Seal were cleaning glasses and he said to Jack "See you soon pineapple face." Lou piped up and said, "Don't give him a big head." Outside it had stopped snowing and there was a light peppering of snow on the ground. "C'mon Jim," said Jack, "We'll take my car." Jack drove a black Cadillac and the chromed finned rear tail lights came into sharp focus. Jim noticed Jack's plates were Californian, Carrie get out your case. In the meantime Lou jumped in the front beside Jack and Jim was content with the rear view. They shut the doors with an expensive clunk. Jack fired up the engine with a low burble and they were off. Jack put the wipers on to clear the windshield of snow. Jim realized pretty quickly that Jack was a great driver,he handled the large automobile like a young girl in her slip. Jack put on the radio and pretty quickly the car was warm. Lou could smell the moist exhaled breath of Alcohol from Jack. He said there was a shooting just here last week it was nearly a fatality. Jack pointed to a liquor store with bright red and white neon Michelob sign. "It was a holdup the assailant was wounded with gunshot." He said. The roads were pretty quiet and Jack speeded up to thirty miles an hour. They were now downtown in Eugene and drove past the red neon of the Hilton. There was more than darkness in the depths and it was exciting getting a drive from Jack. The radio was on an AM station, it was music and the song playing was Sky fall by Diana Ross.

Pretty soon they were in the college. Lou let the electric window down a little and threw away the butt of her cigarette. She zipped up the window and said to Jack, "Are you still building houses in Southern Ca. Jack?" Jack started laughing and said, "That venture in Ventura was a disaster. This Texan East coaster wasn't cut out to build houses,"."God dam feet and inches" piped in Jim. "Degrees Radians Grads sort of thing," said Jack deflated like". . . I lost $2 million". . . "Jack!" Said Lou. She wasn't riding shotgun for nothing.

Pretty soon they were at the Cameo Can cinema it was situated between the Red Rooster barber's pole and Powell's bookstore. The neon above the entrance colored in the first movie coming on Friday the Boxing Day; Miracle on 37th street. Jack parked up in his usual place. They all got out and he locked the central locking. "Books!" Shouted the little twiggy Lou. "Are you still writing poetry?" said Jack laconically. "Yes," said Lou shyly looking into the distance. Jack nodded at Jim and said, "Is valentine may proving a good muse." "Yes," said Lou firmly- "I've grown out of DH Lawrence," said Lou. "I'm married now." "Take one partner and stay healthy," said Jack sagely. Both Jim and Lou had enacted the myth of free love in the past and hopefully they were lovingly content with one another now. Jack had lit a cigarette and said, "I used to think DH Lawrence was the main man Jim I have read all his books several times but now funnily enough I have changed. I turned to Scots writers James Kelman in particular. He captures the alienated bleakness of postindustrial Scotland," said Jack. "Yes," said Jim and he suddenly felt worried at the thought of that man in the caste at Glasgow airport. Louise went over and put her arm around her husband's waist. Jack realized the moment and said, "Quietly C'mon kids let's go inside and get warm." He put his arm around Jim's shoulders and they all went inside to the picture house.

It was nice and warm inside the theater. Jack said Clay was a business partner managing the cinema for him. He shouted loudly "Clay" and a young American African appeared as if from nowhere. Clay had a clubfoot and you could tell he limped a bit. Fucking Lord Byron whispered Jim to Lou and Lou kicked Jim sharply to shut up. Jack said to Lord Byron these are my cousins "Clay we're going to watch a few movies up in the cine room." Clay said easily, "It's all set up in there." Clay put on a light so Jim and Lou could see the theater. It was a posh cut glass chandelier and the Parisian feeling was counterpane by the Mexican reliefs on the wall of cactus and Sierra Nevada. Clay introduced himself, Jim replied, "There is a Prince Of Wales with Mexican relief's like these ones in Aberdeen in Scotland where I come from. "Huh," said Clay, "Small world". Clay said with outspread arms, "What do you think kids this is my little baby." "It's a great little theater," said Jack. There was about a hundred bucket seats in the little amphitheater and there was a bar at the rear that sold beer and dogs. "It's tremendous," said Jim, he had never seen a picture house like this in Scotland. The feeling was laid back and intimate. Clay said, "I love your accent Jim don't lose it" .". . Well enjoy the movies Lou and Jim," and he said he was locking up and going home for the night. Clay and Jack had a brief conversation about business, meanwhile Lou led Jim and they went through the back door and up the stairs to the cine room. Jack shouted, "I'll be with you in a moment kids, grab a beer from the refrigerator." The cine room was small and dark-in the corner was a refrigerator full of Blue Sail amber beer. It was one of Cousin Jack's microbrewery beers. It tasted great thought Jim,light and refreshing. The cine machine was switched on and micro lights glowed in the semi darkness. Lou said, "I think we are alone now Jim you can kiss me if you want to." Jim kissed his wife fully on the lips. Lou looked around there was a stack of film cans against one wall on a rack. She went and looked at the titles and said, "There is lots of stuff here. There's the new Warren Beatty film Bugsy here," said Lou. "Yeah," said Jim, "cool!" Jim turned on a light and looked at the cine machine, he realized you had to synchronies the sound with the motion picture the cine machine. It was an expensive bit of kit and was made by Kodak.

The room was warm and smelt of nothingness. Pretty soon Jack appeared up the stairs and said, "Good you got a beer then. Good."

Jack came and sat down after he had got himself a beer. He said, "Do ye want to smoke some reefer Jim and Lou?" Oh no thought Jim not cannabis resins. But no it was fine. Lou spoke for both of them and said, "yeah we could." "Okay," said cousin Jack who pulled out a joint of pure bud and lit up. Jack meant it in love. How can you articulate drugs thought Jim? He soon found he liked marijuana as much as he detested cannabis resin. It was smoked as a light fire-that's all. Just a taste. Pretty soon all three of them were mildly stoned-green bud thought Jack you can't go wrong. Lou and Jack got into a conversation about Kerouac versus Camus,do we really live in a godless society. A society in which churches of the world are coming together all over the world. "Christianity is sinking its roots into meaningful culture," said Jack, "And my sister is a wolf bite." "I love you cousin Jack, "said Lou and they stood and embraced.

Jack went and found them a movie. Jack said, "This movie is about the genius of Pink Floyd. It's a live performance of "The Wall" made in Belfast in 88'." Wow said Jim, "The Dark side Of The Moon," is one of my favorite albums from teenage years. "Time" is one of my favorite tracks," said Lou. Jack looked at them both and took a suck on his Jaffrey's. He really hoped that they would stay together they were an incredibly sexy couple. "Well LL d'ye want to see some movies" said Jack. Jim said, "Lisa is Lou's second name right enough,LL Cool Jesus Jack." "She's with the right man Jesus" said Jack.

Jack had just about finished rigging up the Cine for the movie. Lou looked at him with a twinkle in her eye and said "Are yeah planning on getting married to her then Jack?" He looked back at her with a second eyed skeil, one brown disc placed partially on Well I'm in love okay. "She has thick black/red wavy hair and an indigo eyed beauty. What's more she's the finest chef in Europe. She's 51, Gemini, half Scots and Moroccan and she's well . . . Jacks." Jim was smoking an Old Gold and was fiddling with his hands, he suddenly asked Jack-"Have you got your ride yet!" "Well hell no" said Jack stoned like." There's the small question of her husband". . . "Fuck it Jack," said Lou "You really are a daft old duck". "Well I love her Lou and that decide that." Said cousin Jack "So what are you going to do bad boy" said Jim. "I'm going to marry her," said Jack bravely. "All's fair in love and war". . . Lou went and cuddled Jack and kissed him on the cheek, she stood back and said tenderly, what does her husband do. "He's an Architect Lou,it was on my real estate misadventure in LA that I met Jacqueline" said Jack. "Bob is one of the most boring men I have ever met in my life; but he's tough, he is from Derry in Northern Ireland." "How does Jacks feel about you Jack," said Louise "It was love at first sight," said Jack. "She has two teenage kids," said Jack "But somehow . . . well I feel I am bound for glory." Where does she live Jack? Said Jim. She lives in Knightsbridge in London," said Jack, "Where about in Scotland is she from Jack?" Said Jim. Dundee said Jack, "Scum Dee" said Lou, she must be cool. "LL cool Jesus," said Jack, "just like the weather- She's a Clarke".

Lou went and sat down beside her husband and thought silently to herself. She had seen Jack fighting in The Blue Moon in Portland,against that Hell's Angel Doggie Maitland,Jackie was a Southpaw and had a mighty left on him, but Doggie had grabbed him and went in with the feet. She looked at Jim-perhaps he could help Jack out in his love quest.

CHAPTER THREE

I awoke in a dazzle. Lou was not beside me. I heard this scurrying noise and I concentrated on the scratching animal running across the polished timber floorboards, it was Bill's armadillo. I looked quickly at its shell of bony plates as it disappeared into the kitchen. We were staying at Connor Mackenzie's apartment and Bill was Connor's flat mate. I was in Portland,we had driven down yesterday. Lou came back from the John, her face was ashen, she told me that she had thrown up. I looked at the russet bristle of her kite and felt aroused, not today Josephine! Lou quickly got dressed and went into the kitchen to make some coffee for us. The armadillo must have gone to ground because I didn't hear Lou scream.

I suddenly thought about the events of last night . . . Connor was an artist; he was from Glenfiddich in Fife Scotland. He was on a year's traveling Scholarship to Portland Institute of Fine Art, (Mark Rothman). I stretched to get an old gold. Bill's lighter was lying on the floor. It had a relief on the front of a naked woman and if you rubbed her naked breasts the nipples glowed red and it sparked up. I took a grateful lungful.

Lou came through from the Kitchenette, she had made Americana's,blue jeans and chinos. I badly wanted to fuck Lou, but she demurred. She said she was getting her period. I respected Lou; boy did I respect Lou. We had met Matt Gere last night . . . He was Lou's last boyfriend before she had come over to Scotland,and me. A horn hooted outside. Matt was syrupy and he had drooled over Lou all night. Enough to say I was jealous of him, he had punctured our safe little bubble. He was virtually slivering all over Lou and I felt like banging him in the mouth,but I had said and done nothing.Lou wasn't his little toy anymore. She seemed to like it.

Have feelings for Matt Gere still, he was the All American hero; He had left the Marines and trained as a Tao therapist and it was his destiny to have become a millionaire here in Portland Oregon. With his black brown eyes. Perhaps it was the grass and the brews but I suddenly remembered Matt and how he looked like Jim Morrison. The entire papoose American girlfriends,in a city where as Courtney Love from Corvallis discovered it is pretty easy to get your hole in the Satyricon nite club any night of the week. Was I done with that way of life now? I wondered about Europe.

I looked at Jim; I still had a buzz on from last night,he looked pretty pissed,sucking on his cigarette. Jim looked at me with his knowing picket turquoise eyes. He burnt two holes through me.It was the first time I had ever refused Jim sex. Jim extinguished his cigarette and got up from the divan couch, he felt like a bust settee; he was coiled. He pulled on his jocks and quietly got dressed.

Connor came through from his bedroom; he was wearing a semmet and a pair of cowboy boots. His face was grizzly and his handlebar moustache bristled. Jim burst out laughing and said in a mock Geordie accent "wyes aye Connor sleep well then." Connor replied in mock Geordie "Slept like the proverbial kitten." Lou was all happed up in the bed drinking on her Americana. Connor looked amongst the detritus of the table and lit up the butt of a stogie with straight stubbed fingers using the lighter left by Bill. Connor went into the kitchenette and looked in the refrigerator. He pulled out the carcass of a chicken that he said Bill had left in there for over a week. "I'll make some soup with this tonight," he murmured from behind his moustache as Lou simultaneously cowked. Jim started laughing as he tried to banish the thought of Matt Gere from last night. It was worrying though,Lou was an American girl and Matt's machismo had excited her. Connor had fixed himself a glass of wine and came and sat on the chair opposite the settee. A strong smell of bovine perspiration coming his flaccid body permeated the room. Connor picked up a spinning fishing reel that had been sitting on the table and he started playing with it. Connor was a keen game fisherman and he had got Jim interested in fishing back in Scotland. He said to Jim that he was hoping to make it up to Alaska on this trip to fish for steel heads, Arctic Char. Jim said this is the season for them Connor. Connor replied back solemnly "correct."

Lou suddenly leapt out of the bed, she had finished her Americano, she gathered up her clothes. Her jeans, white tee shirt, black bra and panties. She made a dash for the bathroom where she locked herself in. Connor remarked silently, "Fuck sakes Jim what a body."

Jim said to Connor conspiratorially that guy Matt that was here last night was Lou's boyfriend here in Portland before she came to Scotland. "I don't like that . . . hem she's married to me now." Connor replied in a deep Fife accent "What you are really trying to say Jim is that you are jealous of him." "I suppose so," said Jim in a small voice looking sadly at the floor. "Her view of America is crystallized Jim," said Connor. "It will all work out in the end." Connor was two years older than Jim and he was more experienced in people although like Jim essentially innocent.

Jim rose and looked out of the window of the apartment. It was an American view; flacked black tar pitch of a flat roof extended ahead and the steam rose in the cold. December morning from stovepipes peppered across the roof. Connor cheered things up and said "Lets go down to the Blue Moon for breakfast." Connor went and got dressed and Jim tidied up the fold down settee.

Lou came back from the bathroom and Jim said to her, "We're going down to the Blue Moon for breakfast." "C'EST la," said Lou in her soft but constant American accent. She really was an unusual girl thought Jim she was American but spoke fluent French learnt from her mother.

Lou was putting moisturizer on her face followed by pan stick. Jim loved watching Lou put on her make up. He watched Lou intently as she put kohl on her eyes and applied a tube of bud No 7 lipstick to her lip smackers. Lou looked at Jim with mirth in her eyes and kissed him on the cheek. Jim went to the bathroom and took a piss. His urine smelt fermented what with watering the liver last night. He washed and rinsed his face in the streams of cold water from the faucet. He suddenly remembered a lecture he had had at university about water. Oregon had the model hydroelectric scheme of both America and Europe,it was fascinating.

So they wound up in the blue moon, one of cousin Jacks bars. Outside there were juvenile larch trees sunk into the ground in square round cupolas and the thought made Jim think of Thomas Berkley and also the antique gold and opal ear studs he had given Lou as an engagement present. Down and across the road from the neon "Highland Mac" sign and the soda fountain. It was a gentile hippy concentric Jim Morrison establishment with pool table and darts board.

Camel red and a cherry coke.

She had on her blue wool coat,she is just eighteen. Lou knew Jewel and Connor perked up when he saw the fragile jack eyed beauty. Lou had met Jewel a few times; at Northwest parties here in Portland and also up in the High street café in Eugene. Jewel was always broke and searching for crumbs.

Lou said to Jewel, "Still singing then-I see you have your guitar with you." (Jewel had once had a one night stand with Matt Gere when he had been seeing Lou) This was all unknown to Jim and Connor although it was true to say that Jim noticed that Jewel had the same nose as him (Robert Graves).

Connor ordered some drinks-this was a microbrewery pub after all. The barman came over and started a tab for Connor. "We'll have three terminator stouts and a coke for the child."

The bar was empty at this time of the day and Jim had a walk around the semi darkness to check it all out. There were pictures of the Grateful Dead over all the walls and various pictures of other bands. Jim stopped at a portrait of Mick Jagger and Keith Richards, Keith looked bored somehow.

Beside the darts board was a portrait of the Queen; Jim knew from Matt Gere last night that the British had sold Oregon to the USA and that there was strong links here. Jim lit up an Old gold with a match from his book and considered the flip top monkey at the bar.

Jim had a strange dream last night. He had dreamt that he had stepped up over and into a warm diesel fumed warehouse back in Britain, through the man hatch, and he had come across a young couple being cruel to their child. The concrete floor of the building was covered in deep and shallow pools of water. The Kid's name was Pepe. Jim had confronted the couple about their cruelty and meanwhile the toddler had drowned itself in one of the pools of water. Jim had tried to revive Pepe but he was dead. Then he woke up. Chilling.

Jim went back over and resumed his place in the "Monday morning club." Jewel had picked up her guitar and was strumming a song. Connor was dying to sing a song.

Louise told Jim quietly that Jewel was originally from Utah but she had been raised around the bar scene in Anchorage Alaska by her mum.

Lou continued to Jim, "It's not unlike Aberdeen, all Klondike's, green velvet crabs and black gold." Jim took a drink of his stout-it tasted rough.

Jewel was singing "Dignity" by Bob Dylan. Connor knew the words and pitched in. Jim looked to the floor, as he was wont to do and noticed Jewel's cowboy boots, they were beautiful black and white hand tooled leather. Jewel was wearing a black denim skirt.

Lou took Jim's hand and said, "Your hands are so scarred darling covered in scars," "That reminds me," said Jim . . . suddenly thinking about the ghastliness of Aberdeen. "The Inuit and St. Nicholas of Anchorage. The patron saint of sailors."

"Lou why were you coming on to Matt last night? You are my wife my love." "I dunno Jim . . . It was a powerful relationship you know-if Jim, you can't accept that well you can't accept change." "I know that sexual values are governed by human behavior Lou-that here the people fuck more other but all the same your view of America doesn't have to be crystallized like Vladimir Nabokov and Lolita."

Jewel had stopped singing and put down her guitar. "I was busking on the door last night and two MC members came in to see Jack; but he wasn't here." Lou suddenly felt concern-so did Jim-his middle name was Macleod after all and he was an old gold shining sun. The Kittiwakes scraked in the background, outside near here and free and cart wheeling the same old story.

"I talked to them when they came back out," said Jewel. "One of them was mountain dew Bob Zapata from the Oakland chapter, that's Oakland Ca. Jim." "What did Bob say," said Lou. Jewel laid her guitar against the bar and lit up a camel. Connor noticed her Robert Graves nose as the young artist took a toke and exhaled a blue gray flume. She pulled the ubiquitous black cup USA ashtray close to her and wedged her camel into one of the seven furls. A car peeped mournfully outside; the evil chorus of evil. Jewel began,

"Steve Munro is dead, He's Bob's son by Cher Indiana Hite the Sioux redskin chick from Montana." Lou inhaled quickly and let it out like a burst tire. "Steve Munro is dead!" said Lou "I can't believe it, he is soul man, rain germ". "Was," said Connor deadpan in finest Fife. "He dropped dead of a heart attack in his sleep", said Jewel as she tapped the ash from her camel lite and took another toke. Lou muttered slightly to herself "Jewish faced little cunt", she had tweaked his nose once at a party in Eugene when he was taxiing for TODA,

Jim had been listening and said intuitively; "So Bob blames Jack for the death of his son." Jewel started laughing, she said, "Steve was bourgeois, he was educated at Stanford same year as Chelsea Clinton, he took a masters in European Literature." Lou thought for a moment and smiled at Jim, she looked at Connor who was draining the fag end of his Terminator stout and said, "He thought he was going to be the next Arthur Miller." "Death of a Salesman," said Jim. Then everyone started laughing hoarsely. Jewel stubbed out her Jimmy

Dean and said, "Bob is an agnostic he just believes in American Spirits he thinks that Jack laid bad Karma on Steve because he fell out with Steve in The High Street Café in Eugene; I was there." What did Jack say?" said Lou, concerned for her uncle. Connor had ordered another round of Terminators and a coke for Jewel. "Well," said Jewel. "Let me tell you," on her high horse. "Jack had been standing at the bar like a real hipster he was talking to the David Russell guy the civil engineer about real estate." Lou butted in and said "You mean Piltdown man," "Yeah that's the fur trapper and Steve was standing on his own at the long Lignum Vitae bar, and He was drinking shots."

The bar was beginning to fill up now a few punters had come in drinking on the papoose.

"Jack posed David a question," said Jewel he told him that the coy he worked with were owned by the Laws of London England, that Jack's Grandfather had worked for them as a Laborer laying sewers in the summer of 56' up in Seattle." Well.can I tell you all Piltdown David was astounded by this piece of information? That Jacks grandfather had owed the coy. Yet Jack."

"David was so taken aback," said Jewel, "That he turned back to his small town mentality; he wouldn't even take Jack's cell phone number.Jack had just proved that he or his family weren't part of that nepotistic bullshit," added Jewel. Jim was interested now,he had met many civil engineers in his time,the only one he had any time for was Steve Lang of St. Andrews. Jim thought about Steve for a moment, he was a scratch golfer and a graduate of Bell Street

College in Dundee, there was something special about Dundee all right; the women were beautiful. Quite frankly Steve couldn't give a fuck,it takes a long spoon to sup with a Fifer. Jim looked at Connor. Connor was simultaneously drinking on his terminator and staring at Jewel's wonderful breasts. Lou piped up and said, "So what happened with Steve and Jack." "Well let me tell you," said Jewel on her high horse. Connor had lit an Old Gold and was cleansing the drips of Terminator from his moustache.

"Steve wired cousin Jack in," said Jewel. "He bought him a Scotch whisky a Talisker I think it was,malt." "Jack owns the god dam bar!" said Lou. "I know," said Jewel in a moment. "But cousin Jack's an unusual man; there was one time in here when Jack had a booth he tried to order some food and the waiter said to him, "I'm not your waitress." "Poor old Cousin Jack," said Lou", the slow but quick witted one." "Well anyhow," said Jewel, she sat back in her seat drew her coke to her and began, "Well let me tell you, Jack had recently moved to a cottage in Garterly in Clackamas County where he was writing his first true novel, THE COMING." I've read that novel "said Connor." It's brilliant but it isn't written under his name; it's written under the pseudonym of Jake Beatty." "It's set around the Satyricon in Portland where the toilet is a bath tub, "Fucking hole," said Lou under her breath. Connor said, "The plots about Gil Scott Heron who eventually is bitten by Banes. "How sad," said Jim ironically." Gil Scott Heron's father was the first black footballer to play for Celtic." Said Connor. "Boston Celtic? Said Lou," Nah dinnae be daft Lou," said Connor. "Glasgow Celtic!"

Jim had started on his second Terminator and was all ears now, he thought about the sniffing around Balfour Beatty engineer he had sent packing when he had befriended Lou on one of her trips through the Kelvingrove park on her evening and morning route as a Bookseller with WH Smith when they lived in 36 Otago Street in Glasgow's west end.

"Well let me tell you," said Jewel, "Steve was blasted at the route he also lived in Garterly in the old church in the graveyard, "Jewel started giggling now she couldn't stop, Lou started giggling as well, Connor said "C'mon get on with it Jewel." She stopped giggling then started again. Lou said, "Have you seen your analyst recently Jewel?" Jewel began again, "Steve had tried to write but he wasn't exactly Walt Whitman he had heard that cousin Jack was writing a book and he was green with envy. He said to Jack that a close neighbor of Jack's wasn't happy that he was staying there. A real moan it was He wouldn't tell Cousin Jack who the neighbor was who wasn't happy with Jack. Steve and Jack had form they had fallen out a few years ago, it was like a red rag to a bull. Cousin Jack hooked him with a left hook and Steve fell into the font well amongst the beer slops and the cigarette butts." "Quite right" said Connor he should have taken his legs off for bad mouthing him in that Irish bar. "Cousin Jack was thrown out for hitting the little punk," the good folk of Eugene weren't used to that kind of subterranean home sick blues." Lou said, "So cousin Jack was left wondering who the close neighbor who didn't like him"... "Correct," said Connor,

Calum Cumming

CHAPTER FOUR

They drove back to Eugene later that day. It was Christmas on Thursday. Lou was driving and Jim settled into the depressing 3 clicks trip up i5. They were on i5 and Jim noticed a small brown dog running up one of the fields trying to keep up with the traffic. He was totally free and there were no humans around. Jim said to Lou," look at that feisty little fellow he's wonderful", Lou replied noticing the dog," He is exempted from duty he's clean that little guy".

Jim had the radio on AM and it was a Eugene station on the channel. It was reported that a pensioner had driven 5 miles the wrong way down the freeway until she was killed by a lorry; wild. Lou said, "You have to watch out for those old guys." Lou said, "Lets stop for some lunch it'll soak up the terminators," Jim said, "Okay darling I'm up for that." Just as they were about to turn off the freeway a possum ran across both lanes of the freeway and Lou killed the rat outright. She was non-plussed, pitiless just like Aeneas when he shows no pity to Tournus and puts him to the sword. "Food for the hooded crows they practice a dance of death on the freeway," Said Lou. They stopped at Denny's diner and parked up the little old silver Toyota. They got out of the car and had a hug, it was mild yet cold a curious combination,a dry cold. Jim looked at Lou and saw her in a new light. That little scar above her left eye; she was older than me in spirit. In a tick he felt like a destitute institute and somehow he realized that Lou had allowed the Hughie Morgan of Portland, Matt Gere to re-enter her life-polluting their lives. This is just ridiculous he thought. They broke apart and Jim followed Lou into the Diner.

It was pretty quiet and they took a booth. There was tinsel placed outside the diner and a Christmas tree inside a vast continent of sweeping loneliness, what would I do here without Lou.I had sent for all the forms from immigration and naturalization so I could get an amber card, amber gambler I thought, where was Madonna my old American friend from Aberdeen now . . . I was a guest in this country. They sat down and Lou looked at the menu nonchalantly. The waitress came over with the coffee percolator and they both had coffee with half and half and white sugar. Jim looked at the menu.He decided on roast beef with biscuits and gravy-The waitress came back over her face looked like one of those old airline stewardesses, living on a diet of high carbohydrate food and Senna. She had kind tired professional eyes it punctuated her hardness. Lou settled for the enchiladas and stuck out her tongue cheekily as she was won't to do as I ordered my Roast beef and gravy. Jim was looking forward to his gravy!

There was a young couple sitting in booth on the other side of the aisle, he was wearing a blue rayon and cotton windcheater outside his orange wool sweater. Airily. Lou leaned over conspiratorially and said, "They've just come back from LA." Jim asked Lou what time was jimmying arriving at her parent's home Swiss Cottage. "He'll be here tonight," said

JACK NICHOLSON

Lou. Jim wondered if he was some kind of chief executive driving a Pontiac Continental. He sat back on my couch, the guest addressing the patron. She had pulled out her compact and Revlon lipstick,she was oblivious to me. She really was stunning she could have made it in Hollywood as an actress or a supermodel I thought-what a pussycat. I wanted to poke her.

The waitress came across with the food.Lou's enchiladas looked delicious and I stared with growing dismay at my own fare. I was crestfallen. The waitress refilled our coffee cups laid the tab on the table and said emptily "enjoy." Lou wished her a merry Christmas and she replied, "You're welcome,enjoy." She disappeared round the corner to the diner bar. My gravy looked like gissum it was white and the beef was like thin leather, the biscuits were like brown buttons. Lisa laughed naughty "You have to watch those guys." "I wanted meat gravy" I said to Lou "Not this glutinous crap," "its cornflower," said Lou that's what we call gravy in USA.

I picked at my food and ate all the beef. Lou laughed "You'll remember not to have that again in Denny's diner Totem pole" They paid the bill and left-they had somewhere to go a home waiting for them. Jim listened to the tinsel metallically swishing in the wind and he wondered what LA was like. Was it like the cornflower gravy-white and glutinous and of no nutritional value?

They arrived at Swiss cottage at 3pm or thereabouts. There was a wreath of holly hanging on the door. They sat in the car for a minute and smoked. Jim said to Lou "I remember once in

Brechin in the farmyard at newforebank my grandfather Jim lit a fire in frosty January and threw on the holly Christmas tree-it burned bleak green flames-the wood. The heat of the fire burnt it and Jim was cackling to himself". "Burn Holly,weird burn," replied Lou. She had smoked her cigarette right to the butt and threw the butt out the window. They went in.

Jude was making French bread in the kitchen, and Ned was down in the den watching NBA Midwestern league. It was nice and warm. BJ must have been in her room watching film noir. "Well hello there you two," said Jude happily. She was relieved to see us back in one piece. "Jimmy will be here around 7pm he called from the motel at lake Shasta." Lou helped herself to some orange juice and said, "I'm away to have a shower Jesus I have a headache." "There's Tylenol in the bathroom honey," "Sure mom," replied Louise haughtily. Jim helped himself to some coffee and sat and talked to Jude.

"Jimmy lives in Hollywood right," said Jim, "What's it like there." Jude looked at Jim with serious eyes, he was a novice she thought but she decided to fill him in with some of the details of Hollywood. "There are a lot of people with bruised souls who live in Hollywood." Jude fixed herself some Lipton's hot lemon tea and came and sat with the gamest loser in the world. "I remember back in 62 just before I met Ned I was working as a nurse in the cedars Sinai hospital,it was the day that Marilyn Monroe died and I walked past her house. The widow was wide open and the magenta curtain swished in the wind. It was dark in there real dark . . . There is every kind of farm help and horny handed laborer from all over

America in Hollywood,all trying to make it in the fame game." "Jimmy lives in one of the starlet colonies apartments in Swail drive-just beside Rodeo drive" Jim said, "Have you seen Chinatown,it shines golden water coming from the shower faucet- just like one of the golden girls." "No I haven't seen that movie," said Jude. Rents are cheap in Hollywood if you decide to settle there, "of course" said Jim. "I remember when Ned and I first married Ned worked as a parking lot attendant in West Hollywood off the boulevard and he used to park the stars cars,he used to park Laurel and Hardy's cars". Jude took a sip of her Lipton's hot tea. She went on," He used to park Peter Lawford's car,one of the rat pack,and Ned said he watched him go downhill with drink." Jim thought about a Scots poem The Thistle and the Rose and said, "The private should mirror the public," "While at the same time looking after your wife," said Jude. "There a lot of the stars that suffer from mental illness," said Jude. "Look what happened to Sam Shepherd's Frances Farmer," said Jude. "Stick with your Garrison Keillor meantime Jim lake Woebegone days"... "Yes" replied Jim diffidently.

Jimmy arrived round about 7pm,he was driving an old bronze Honda jazz and it was the first time he had visited Swiss Cottage. He didn't even knock and walked straight down and into the den. Ned and Jim were watching the NBC news about an incident in LA. A white lorry driver Rodney King had been arrested and assaulted by the police in South Central LA,it was to prove to be a catalyst for the LA riots,the worst incidence of break down in law and order in the USA since the notorious Watts riots in 1968.

Jimmy introduced himself to Jim. Jimmy shook his hand weakly. He was wearing turquoise lake contact lenses,obscuring his watery gray blue eyes. He had a golden wave,like James Kirkup,thought Jim, and he was lightly tanned. He spoke in a pseudo Southern drawl. Jimmy had proved to be a real disappointment to Ned, he was gay and he liked to be the man in relationships. Ned said to Jimmy and Jim "Looks like there is going to be trouble in LA it was aunt Hope calling from Glendale California". Aunt Hope, Jude's sister was a real character she was retired as a jeweler salesman with Tiffanies of Rodeo drive and Lou had told Jim about her. Hope had been a real beauty back in the day and the year love of her life had been Warren Tiffany, He was married and she had been content with putting the shop goods in the window all her adult life. Lou had told Jim that Hope was 75 and smoked 40 Camel lites a day and she had burnt all the hair off the inside of her nose with the coke. Ned had said to Hope "Jimmy's here he just arrived-Jim's settled in fine and we're going to the range tomorrow to hit balls it's all about getting to the dance floor Hope." Jude picked the phone up upstairs in the study and spoke to her older sister Hope in a tick. Jude called Louise, Hope was dying to speak to her favorite niece.

Jimmy sat down for a moment and replied, "This is a really wonderful house Pops". Jimmy was already eying up what was in this trip for him. On the question of credibility Jim's family on his father's side were the first family of Edinburgh and Jim never thought about the benefits of that. Jim was from old money-upper middle class although back in Scotland he had a liking for the "low class curry". A rich mix of trash this guy was the immediate conclusion Jim had formed about this amoral LA sociopath with his fake eyes. "Ho hum" said Jimmy and went up to the kitchen-he already fancied Jim. Lou had been lying down and Jim heard over the NBC bulletin Jimmy talking to Jude.

Lou came into the kitchen from the phone to Hope-her time is now bleeding and she had changed her little white mouse Lillet. Lou embraced Jimmy coldly she couldn't stand him he knew how to rain on the parade, for no particular reason she disliked her own flesh and blood. Lou said to Jimmy, "Hi toots you made it up alright," she hadn't seen Jimmy for over three years and she couldn't think of anything to say to him except, "nice contacts Jimmy."

Jimmy went into the freeze and helped himself to some roast ham, butter and bread and the four cans of Coors that Jim had picked up. Lou watched him intently. She thought he was so selfish that he would drink the last drop of milk before the rest of the family got any, fucking social climber Cyril Connolly in the rock pool. Louise said, "Are you still going for sweat weekends in the desert Jimmy?" Male bodies entangled and writhing like prison spaghetti at Abu Grab. "Whatever it takes to take one step forward and two back Jimmy," said Lou, She thought about Jimmy's claim to fame-he had had an affair with the artist David Hockney and had ended up attacking him with a pair of scissors when in a tick David had dropped him for a Spanish mateador. "Ho hum" said Jimmy as he finished his sandwich and took a long slug from one of Jim's Coors. "We're putting you in the den Jimmy," said Jude. Jimmy lit a Rothman's blue with a burp and said, "That's fine Mom."

Jimmy said, "I'm away for a shower Mom," and he disappeared with his bag and can of Coors to the downstairs bathroom. Jimmy went in and locked the door-he took a piss with his circumcised American cock-he had a brown purple wine stain on the shaft of his cock-it was a birthmark. He zipped up and put away his large phallus. He was wearing white Calvin Klein briefless pants,like Pablo Picasso. He fished in his bag for all his bottles of tablets and lay them open on the bench above the John below the lowlight surround mirror. He couldn't find his Quaaludes he had found the Demerol and the Valium but he couldn't find his Quaaludes. He searched frantically amongst the open bottles of capsules with his scratching jealous nails. It had become a struggle. Jim heard the noise and thought feisty, "Him weak man would destroy almost everything around him." Jimmy took out his phial and settled for a line of coke chopped with his blockbuster video card. Jimmy was seeing soft pink rabbit colors now and he settled for a shave. He ran the hot and cold faucets and placed one of Jim's disposable razors in the warm Oregon water. He liberally applied shaving cream from the cinnamon barbasol that stood cheaply on the ledge and Jimmy had a hot shave. After Jimmy had finished shaving he looked in the mirror and said softly to himself, "You know who he is."

Upstairs in the kitchen Louise told Jude she had her period and she felt terrible. "It's a river that runs in you honey," said Jude. "I had a bloody coil put in back in Scotland said Louise, "Jim doesn't mind". Jude looked at her daughter sagely and said,

JACK NICHOLSON

"When the time is right you'll have your babies". Lou thought for a moment she had an abortion in the twelve grades to an LA cop,they used to ball in the hi6 motel in Silver Lake,he used to lay his gun and shoulder holster on the bedside cabinet but she had smartly never told Jude about the LA cop or the ensuing abortion. Louise replied to Jude taciturnly, "The last turn of the screw Mummy dearest."

The next day Ned and Jim went to the range and drove skins. It was a bright warm misty rising day. Jim was still tired.Lou had been crying last night at bedtime. Jim was dying for a sup of his wife but she settled for some hot milk, Tylenol and cookies.

The range was almost empty and Jim looked round the pro shop. Ping irons a full bag was retailing for less than $600 they would cost more than £1000 in Scotland. Ned bought a box of "Wilson" pro flite balls for ten dollars. Jim and Ned went and got some striped balls from the machine with a ratatattat into their buckets and hit fifty skins for a dollar each. Jim watched the only other player on the range. He was driving skins 300 yards or further-amongst the pall with street shoes on. Jim found it hard to swallow- the guy could hit as far as Mannie Daly straight. Jim said to Ned, "Look at that guy." Ned replied, "He's great he's always here when I come it must be about letting out anger or something". The guy noticed Jim and Ned looking at him and shouted out "Straight down the god dam line grand-dad."

Jim was hitting a five iron and he managed to hit the ball 160 yards straight. He hadn't hit a ball for over 2 years but the Macgregor 5 iron was put in his hands so he could get into the zone. Jim hit about 30 balls

or so-Jim only had a three quarter swing on account of his bad back. There were animals coming on the range that looked like large dark brown badgers. Jim said to Ned "what are those critters Ned?"
"They're Nutrias Jim, humans Jim but not as we know them, they are harmless herbivores that you find on the golf courses of Eugene."

Jim felt so happy to be on the range with Ned in the mild northwest pacific winter. It was reciprocated in Ned but he was a quiet man who didn't like to give too much away. Jim watched Ned's swing. He had a light full swing, about 220 yards with a 2 iron and he curved into the skins-although he was prone to hook the ball. He was a par player. It was all about the grip thought Jim-the game of golf gives itself away to you slowly like a good game of chess. It's about friends thought Jim.

Lou liked to play golf she was learning,she had a great swing and it was one of Jim's ambitions to share the excitement of his wife partnering him around the old course in St. Andrews with her sexy bum,pipe dreams. It was almost Christmas and Jim enjoyed the moment with Ned. All to soon they had hit all their balls and the moment was over. It just reinforced in Jim how much he loved America.

Jim and Ned handed in their empty buckets and made their way back to Swiss Cottage in the Toyota Hi-lux. On the way home Ned told Jim a story about his time in the US navy when he had been stationed at ice station Zebra in the North Pole as a conscript during winter in the mid 50s'. "It was bizarre Jim there was no daylight it was the strangest experience of my life. I was on smart watch and I can categorically state that I saw ghosts." Jim replied, "The North frozen soul Ned." "And I was the south frozen son," replied Ned. "The ether in that place are incredible," said Ned it's the only time I have been truly terrified in my life. I wasn't scared of the Russians it was the ghosts that terrified me." Jim said, "My great uncle Calum was on the Arctic convoys in the second world war." "Oh really," said Ned. "He was from another continent but he had been to Archangel and heard the same terrible voices as you Ned," said Jim. Did he survive said Ned the war I mean did he?" "Sure did he wasn't called the battling Mac for nothing."

They got back around eleven. BJ was in the kitchen going into the cabinet for her lithium.I wondered if you could redesign BJ would she still open at the bottom? Lou was in the bedroom putting on her makeup. She said "We're going to the mall today to buy some Christmas presents." "Okay honeysuckle," Jim replied. Louise said, "I've arranged to meet an old friend of mine there his name is Charles Prempeh." "Is he African?" I said. "Yeah" said Lou.

"He's from the other side of the tracks and now he lives on Craigie and Butler. He'll be walking to the mall." "How do you know Charles?" I said slightly taken aback,white kids didn't mix with blacks in America." "I met him at the Eugene Art School prom he was on a mature student Rhodes scholarship there ... he is a genius,as talented as Connor Mackenzie but he's bipolar-his temperament isn't suited for painting" . . . ."Charles never knew his father who was Ghanaian and a doctor. Charles's mother is from Portland,Shirley Buch-she is a nurse; so I guess you can figure out the rest lamb. Charles is Ashanti Roi the Ghanaian royal family who were exiled by Jerry Rawlins. Charles wants to be king himself. His father shot himself in a motel room in Salem city about ten years ago." I replied "I suppose that is real tough and all; is Charles married?" "Ghana is a republic now so I suppose that Charles will always be in exile but yeah Charles is 42 now and married to his childhood sweetheart Joanne Osborne the blimp," said Lou. "Don't look back in anger then," I added. Louise said positively. "Most of Charlie's life has been the full oasis of crap."

Jim went into the kitchen Jimmy was sitting there talking to BJ. Jimmy was wearing a black polo neck lambs wool sweater. The golden wave was still waving-not drowning like Stevie Smith. BJ was waxing about John Wayne I heard Lou hurrying on down to the den to get the latest news about the gathering storm in LA. I sat down and listened to BJ the banger who was in mid conversation. She was having a good morning so far." I used to visit John Wayne every day when he had the guts to face up to lung cancer in that sanctuary of his room in Cedars Sinai in LA." Jimmy lit a Rothmans and exhaled the blue smoke casually "Fucking cunt" I thought. John Wayne was Scots American one of the old Morrison. BJ said, "John didn't like to play against the lower divisions he was a hero right to the end." Jim thought about his father Norman-he had seen action in world war two and Korea. My grandfather Ian came through the 14-18 conflicts as a private in the Royal Artillery regiment. John Wayne the all American hero hadn't fired a shot in anger in his life and yet it was Marlboro red that did for him.

Lou came into the kitchen and said, "Ready Freddy

Mercury?" Fucking bitch I thought I didn't like that comparison,seeing that all comparisons are erroneous anyway.

We drove down to the Mall in Springfield and parked up. "Aha" I thought aloud, "Even the Malls are bigger here." It was called the Sears center. We went in and up the walking stairs to the stores.

The mall was busy with shoppers for Christmas. Lou said, "Let's get Jimmies present out of the way." They went into super drug and Lou bought a bottle of Jojoba Pantene shampoo for Warren Beatty. "That's him out of the way," said Lou. "It'll help to get rid of the smell of second hand pot smoke out of his hair." They then went into Powell's the bookstore and had a good look around, they decided to buy two books for Ned and Jude. There was musak in the mall and there was Bach playing in Powell's. Women, children and the elderly were reading all sorts of books in Powell's. Lou said, "Lets get THE FIRST MAN by Camus for Mom she won't have read it. Can you lend me some dough for the book Jim?" "Okay plum pudding," said Jim The book was a vintage imprint and cost $25. Jim handed Louise the wonga. She stood in line patiently waiting to pay for her book.

Jim went to the sports stand,he was going to get a golf book for Ned. There were plenty of autobiographies and he read a few flyleaves. He decided on THE NINETEENTH HOLE by Sam Torrance,it was a hoot; most of it was set in the pub- amongst the smell of Drum rolling tobacco and Timothy Taylor's Landlord. In a tick Jim joined Lou in line with his book. Jim showed Lou his book. Lou looked at the front of the book and said, "What a sexy dude Jim." The book cost $34. Jim told Lou that Sam's Dad Bob was the most respected coach in the home of golf Scotland. "He's as famous as Butch Harman that old fella." They paid for their books and left with their sack.

They went and sat around the fountain and orange tree deciding what to do next. Lou said "we're not meeting Charles until one thirty we have half an hour to kill" "What will we get BJ?" said Jim. The noise of the thrall and the musak sped things along. "That's easy," said Lou, "she wants a new phone." Jim said, "I'll have to go to the hole in the wall and get some more money." They stood up and went to the Citibank cash machine. Jim withdrew $200 and they then went into the Northwest Bell Pacific phone shop to buy BJ a phone. Lou knew exactly what phone BJ wanted, it was a Viacom cordless ivory. The phone cost Jim $62 which left Jim $138 for Lou's present. We just have time to buy my present said Lou.I know what I want Lou said, "C'mon," and led Jim by the hand. They went into the plaid shop Lou had been wooed by the plaid shop, -not only here but back in Scotland also. She wanted a Macleod of Harris Kilt made by Ralph Lauren. Lou said, "I'm just going to try this on." Lou disappeared into the dressing room. Jim was left amongst the colors of the clans of Scotland. Jim was up for something to eat. Lou came out of the dressing room in her sexy short kilt,she looked fabulous just like one of Tam Paties roller girls. Jim soon had a semi on and he seared with sexual frustration at the sight of his stunning wife. He had goose bumps on his arms and momentarily dropped the phone. "What do you think oatmeal features," said Lou. Jim lifted up the front of his wife's kilt and espied the beautiful curved clump of her mojo defined against her white Per uno panties. "You wear something under your kilt then ginger Peachy." "Of course" said Lou brushing Jim's hand away. "I want it," said Lou "The kilt you mean?" replied Jim. "Of course," said Louise, "What else did you think I meant?"

Jim paid $120 for the kilt and was left with $18 for lunch. The store assistant packed the kilt into an oblong boutique cardboard box just like the salons in Paris France, euro centric America thought Louise. They left the store and went to meet Charles who was standing patiently outside the "London" café waiting for them with his pet border collie Miguel on a lead.

Charles wore brown horn rimmed glasses and he peered over the top of them at Lou and Jim coming towards him. "She's done it again," thought Charles "She's pulled another guy with movie star good looks." Lou hugged Charles and said "Charlie." Jim took his hand and said, "Hi Jim." He bent down and stroked Chic's dog Miguel who was wagging his black and white tipped tail enthusiastically. Lou said, "Lets go in and catch up on your news Charlie." Jim stood up and noticed that Charles was light brown and had a perfectly round skull,a gold coast African- and he also noticed that Chic's face was pitted with acne scars. They went in. Lou saw a window seat where a couple was paying their check.

They soon sat down and looked at the menus. Lou realized that Charlie had had high hopes when he went to Art School and all that had been erased by Bipolar. Charlie said to Jim, "How are you settling in it's a fine sunny day today." Lou said quickly, "There's been a bit of rain recently but we can't complain." Charles said he had a cold. "I really like the States," said Jim "I'm hoping to get my amber card." "That I'll take a while," said Charles hoarsely. Charlie pulled out a crumpled pack of Camels and lit himself up. Miguel looked on with dismay. Lou said, "How did you take it when Salvador Dali died recently?" Lou knew that Dali was his hero. "If only he hadn't married that bitch Gala perhaps he would have painted the picture of Christ kissing Mary Magdalene by now," said Chic. He started hooting with laughter as he spilled ash on to the table. "Sorry Lou," said Charles. Lou started laughing at Charles inimitable laugh. Jim said to Chic "What are you having to eat?" Lou interrupted brusquely and said, "We'll have hamburgers and fries and three strawberry milkshakes." Lou pointed at the kitchen and said, "Go up and order it Jim." He followed his wife's order tamely and went up to the counter. Lou leant towards Charles conspiratorially as Chic spilt more ash on the table. "Sorry Lou" "This is the most exciting day out I've had in weeks," said Charles, "I met cousin Jack this morning when I was at the post office cashing my social check." He told me that he had a problem with one of his neighbors." Charles apologized again for spilling ash and stubbed out the camel. "He's fallen out with Carla Banes." "Oh no" said Lou doing her best impression of Elaine Stritch. "She is the biggest ecstasy dealer on the Portland coast." "Jack didn't look worried," said Charlie. Lou lit up an old gold and leaned even closer to Charlie and replied, "Does she still use the moniker Tanya Siouxneezee? Fucking fish wife." Jim came back from the counter looked at them both and said, "What?"

"Never you mind," said Lou "Did you get the order?" "Sure did sweet pea?" said Jim proudly. He sat down and Chic lit another camel from his crumpled packet. Jim said, "Are you still working or are you retired Charles?" "A gentleman of the road," said Chic hooting with laughter.

Pretty soon the order came over and they ate. Lou gave Miguel some hamburger and fries and he wolfed it down. Little growk thought Jim. Lou said to Charles, "It's tainted my day,the news about Cousin Jack." Charlie was wiring into his burger and said with a full mouth high "Carla got nine months in Newport woman's penitennuary . . . eight years ago." Jim was eating steadily and said to Lou "Jack's neighbor no?" "Fucking drug dealers" said Lou "Cousin Jack grows his own pot." The mystery neighbor now became obvious to Lou Carla was a 55 year old dried up bitch; she'd always been jealous of Jack. Lou remembered when Jack had got a poem published and he was writing a body of work. He had shown Carla some of his other work and she had treated it with derision. She was a fucking bitch, (It takes one to know one), whose only claim to fame was that she had once walked down Rodeo drive and all the stars went into hiding. "Right" said Lou "We'll see about Ms Chic" Charles had finished his burger and fries and said, "No man, Richard Round tree in shaft"

Jim lit a smoke and inhaled gratefully-he was a guest in this country. He looked at Miguel he had a soft pink patch on his nose and he was lying on his side soporifically now the food was finished. It was a victory for carnivores everywhere.

Calum Cumming

CHAPTER FIVE

Jim and Lou dropped off Charles and Miguel and went home to the relative sanctuary of Swiss Cottage. Jude was washing the dishes in the kitchen and said that Ned had bought a frozen turkey. "It's in the freezer in the garage," said Jude. Lou seemed disassociated from reality she said nothing and went into the bedroom with her presents. Jim went into an angry mood with his partner; she hadn't been the same since Portland and Matt Gere. In a tic Jim followed his wife into the bedroom and shut the door. He confronted her with the shocking truth however unpalatable it may turn out to be.

Louise was sitting on the side of the bed sobbing. Jim said to her angrily, "One plus one does not equal three Lou, what did you think you were doing with Matt the other night?" He pointed at her pathetic lie and said loudly "Tu EST UN boot Lou." She replied to Jim in French between sobs "Vous etes UN cunt . . . merde alors-comment ca VA? Leave me alone you bully!" "No I won't leave you alone,if you want to be with me you don't come on to that squeaky voiced Republican ex-boyfriend of yours." Lou replied immediately to Jim's accusation and said "Matt doesn't have a squeaky voice, his voice is sweet sounding,he's from Virginia." "And I suppose you're a vestal virgin," said Jim.

Lou stood up and slapped Jim in the face with her

ring hand. Jim's cheek stung and it made him angrier. Lou stood facing him and said, "We all have a history if you can't handle my American history you absolutely don't deserve to be with me." Jim looked at her,Lou looked beautiful and bewildered. He said cruelly, "You are somebody who wants to be cherished by a Tao twat." Lou started laughing wild eyed and mad. The exchange of angry words was now over although Jim walked out of the room with a loud slam and went down to the Den where Jimmy was lying with a comforter on the casting couch.

Lou thought irrationally she gathered up her cigarettes, make up and her lillets. He's just a waste of time thought Lou.I think I'll do some moonlighting. The anger of her energy drove her on. Onwards ever onwards . . . She put on her Scorpio beat jacket and gathered up the car keys. Lou left quietly and slammed the door of the Toyota Corolla loudly. She turned the keys of the ignition put the car into reverse and was gone to Portland.

"Little marital distress," said Jimmy in his pseudo Southern drawl." "The Mortician Adams has nothing on your clan," said Jim, listening to his errant wife taking off.

Ned came down to the Den he was wearing a yellow Lakers top. He's not quite Magic Mannieson thought Jim. A newsreel came on over the NBC news-Walter Crinite announced solemnly that President George Bush had been taken ill at a Japanese State banquet. He had been sick under the table after eating some dodgy sushi fish. In a tic Ned shouted to BJ to come through from her bedroom. Ned said, "Come through Betsy Joe the President just vomited." Jim thought bitterly it's the only fish I'll be getting tonight.

Lou arrived at Matt's house in about two and a half hours, the poison gas in her had subsided to pure oxygen. Matt lived in Beverly Hills beside Gus van Sant the film director. Matt's bronze Mercedes saloon was sitting in the drive and an old Ford Bronco was parked in front of his substantial wooden property. She went and rang the doorbell. There was an empty chips bag lying at his door, Doritos cheesy chips. Matt came and answered the door. He was wearing a white hoped vest showing off his bronzed rippling muscles and his tattooed arms. Matt was wearing red pants had a close cut goatee beard and moustache. He said in his squeaky voice, "Sweet Marie it's you Lou I didn't think I would cop one with you again," Louise said quickly. "Right; can I come in Matt." "Of course said Matt." Lou looked over her shoulder snippily and went in with that sinking feeling. Matt closed the mahogany full core door without fanfare.

In Swiss cottage they were having dinner there was an empty place for Lou and Ned and Jude said nothing. Betsy Joe was full of malevolent glee for she had never had a relationship with a man in her life and she suffered from arrested development left up on the mantle piece. They were having meat loaf for supper. Time to eat a rock star, I would do anything for love but I won't do that. Ned wolfed down his tasty supper-Jim watched him he was like a little child in the Lego room.

Jimmy toyed with his food; Jim was tired and ratty,he gazed blankly at Jimmy with disgust-like a wicked tiger. He felt like saying fuck off you cunt. Jimmy Jude and BJ drifted down to the den after dinner; the dishes were in the sink.

Ned realized that Jimmy had encountered the Californian "Lotus eater" and he tried to put some spunk in Jim. He recounted, "My partner in Ventura when the kids were growing up was an LA cop. He wound up Captain in Brentwood."

"Jim he is a take no bullshit Irishman; Mannie Fitzgerald." Jim had come down from his disdain for Americans and was interested now. He took a drink of coffee and said "Yeah no shit." "He made a famous arrest in his career," said Jim. "He was one of the arresting officers in the Charles Manson case." Jim shuddered to the base of his spine,everyone knew about Charlie Manson,he was of North east Scots descent,the most notorious living convict in America. Jim had seen a film about Charles Manson the cult of Charlie and the Manson family,his quasi commune and his fucked up little white middle class female Californian acolytes. He was a thoroughly evil man who had butchered with a carving knife the heavily pregnant Sharon Tate-the wife of Roman Polanski the Auschwitz survivor and film director, and the actor Rosemary La Bianca, Sharon's friend. He was found guilty of conspiracy. He had founded the Helter Skelter movement where he believed that society was guilty of racial crimes and there had to be atonement, he was a fringe musician in the La scene and he had befriended the Beach Boy's drummer.

Jim said Dryly in reply to Ned "He fairly descended the spiral that evil little bastard." Ned said, "Mannie arrested him in LA county,he was cowering under a log cabin like a chained dog."

Jim suddenly thought about the old car wash.The American car wash in Aberdeen in Albert street. Round the back of the carwash under the pilings beside the burn was a gravel rough cored open hilly underground basement-dry and dusty. In the summer months Jim and Seamus Morgan used to go there and smoke cinnamon sticks. One day in 1974 there was this older mental case kid who came and sat with them smoking no6 and started spieling off about Planet Of The Apes the latest hit movie, He pulled out his stump and started wanking himself off. Jim had thrown grit at his cock and Seamus kicked him in the face-the kid fucked off. That is how Jim thought of Charles Manson's arrest.

"I hope Mannie hit him before he cuffed him" said Jim. "Yeah he did," said Ned, "He fairly pulled his house of cards down that hot dusty sunny morning Mannie paneled him."

Jim finished his coffee stood up and rinsed the cup and placed it on the draining board.

He stood with his back to the black double window and said, "There is a guy from Aberdeen called Arthur Jackson he used to own a newsagent there-my friend Gary Cumming used to buy his cigarettes there, he was popular with the teenagers on Broomhill road. Jackson was obsessed with Theresa Saldana the New York actress who played Robert De Niro's wife in Raging Bull.Arthur stalked her and tried to murder her in the USA,he was convicted and is serving life in an American jail." "I'm half pict; an

Aberdonian; my beautiful mum Betsy Caird is from Lunan bay north of Dundee-an Irish Pict not a beaker," said Jim. He raised his voice a notch and said, "Some Aberdeen city people are assholes-The beaker people the cod and haddock rans as opposed to the shire Picts-five thousand years of civilization and all the beaker people managed was the clay pot for holding their gold." Ned said slowly "Aberdeen isn't quite Houston Jim but Pict runes is a civilization-a language."

"Where is your heart Jim?" pleaded Ned "We had an argument and she stormed out," replied Jim sadly. "I think she went to Portland." Then Ned looked at Jim honestly and replied from down on his seat "I'm sure Lou will call tonight,it is just one of those problems that needs to be ironed out" .". . Let's go down to the den Jim"

Lou went down and into the split-level living room and open kitchen. McPhail Gere's partner was sitting there,he had on green pants like something out of A&E. The old stereotypes certainly are outdated in this home. McPhail was an actor and painter-he was stoned all the time and was like one of those dumb blonde Californian bimbos on high energy permanently. He had virtually tried to rape Lou once at Northwestern campus and Karen told Lou he had a little tad of a cock-he described Lou as a Swiss type girl-although Mannie had as about as much chance with a European girl as Jim had of getting an erection tonight.

Matt slid into the white leather couch, "We're just about to eat Louise would you like to join us?" Okay said Lou "I'm feeling hungry." The serial hack

McPhail chipped in "we're having Tacos and salad Lou." McPhail took out his pipe and made up a bowl of green bud. Matt brought Lou a large glass of Riesling wine. Lou suddenly thought I have made a dreadful mistake coming here in no way was this progress. Lou thought about McPhail's room at U of O campus, it was a bookless shrine to Harold Lloyd his hero. Lou had once started a fight with him in the Library at Northwest over her black friend Karen Abbott who was forced to terminate a pregnancy because of his serial womanizing and she realized that he was a moral and physical coward, he had zero chance of making it in Hollywood, so he was content with the vapid Art scene of Portland where the true heroes the Hispanics caught the transit. McPhail lit up his pipe and started blowing hard. He then passed the pipe to Matt who equally took a good smoke,Lou declined the pipe she wanted to keep a clear head, which was a good sign. "McPhail this is great bud"" said Gere "It's Louisiana blue Gere" said McPhail. Biff and fucking Happy thought Lou. Gere said slowly in his mellifluous Virginia drawl "You sure look nice Lou I I never saw it before". "You were too busy looking up Jewels skirt she was underage Matt you chased her down to a red light." "I was her Henry Miller said Gere" "What the fuck would you know about Big Sur and The Angels Matt? You leave Jewel the young star out of this. I drove an obstacle course to get here tonight and all you can do is smoke dope." Said Lou. "I'll go and get the dinner said Gere, "The British eat boiled food I can't stand boiled food," He said in defeat. Matt stood and went through to the open plan kitchen and got the beef tacos ready with red Monterey Jack. He tossed the salad with gusto like Reginald Bosanquet. McPhail put some oil of Olay on his psoriasis,ridden hands. Lou looked at his hands he had hands like a lizard.

"McPhail looked at Louise cadaverously and said "I just got the part of the back view for River Phoenix in a movie called my Own Private Idaho, it is about a homosexual relationship between Keanu Reeves and River" "The rear passage view?" said Lou, the irony was lost on McPhail. He had about as much irony as a merchant on Benzedrine. "Gus got me the part". The high priest of the Portland art scene,strictly limited potential, his films were like The Jack London hotel downtown-Mannie barleycorn and urban cowboy speedballs and about to be demolished. Matt called them through to eat, he had put on a blue Ben Sherman button fly shirt. And it hung open.

Lou sat at the head of the table and Gere and McPhail faced off one another, Gere had put on some music Lou realized that it was New Order. Matt had once been to Doncaster to visit an uncle and like Portland white American trash fancied himself as a bit of an aesthete. He topped up Lou's glass with more Riesling. Lou thought Jim would have served a good rioja. She started laughing and really missed Jim's Scots passion. Matt tossed the salad again and Lou said "Does Oscar Wilde here want you Bossy to toss off the salad"-it is lost on both of them and McPhail was attacking his tacos voraciously making an animal noise. Pretty soon they finished dinner and the two heroes went down to the living room for a condor moment. Lou asked Matt if she could phone home. Gere agreed reluctantly for he still cherished secret ambitions that night of using his saveloy sausage. He had been to

Doncaster after all. But he had one chance and that was no chance.

Lou put the call through and got Jude on the telephone.
"Hello Mom it's Louise; I'm at Matt's house in Portland"
"You'd better speak to Jim honey, he's worried sick about you"
"Sure Mom; I'm fine I'll be back in the morning"
Jim went up to the study and took the call from Lou in Portland.
"Aye aye sweetheart are yeah okay is you fine baby"
"I'm sorry Jim I'm at Gere's house, you're right he's an asshole grunt who never even made it to operation desert storm"
"I miss you honey blossom you're my lamb Lou"
"It is just that I had to investigate things to realize how much I care about only you Jim, I'll be back in the morning"
"You take care Lou I'm in a terrible place"
"Trust me sweetheart he means nothing to me He drowns me in paralysis I feel suffocated with his squeaky voice"
"Too much growth hormone Lou, it atrophies the testicles"
"I won't let him near me . . . Jim I have to go now"
Okay Lou I trust you implicitly Porgies"
"Bye Louise Lisa Cumming"
«tseB eyB»

"Hi Jack" said Ned. Ned answered the door and Cousin Jack drifted in and down to the Den he had brought six cold rolling rock beers with him-he put a smile on everyone's face. Jack said "Where's my favorite Valentine May tonight" Jimmy said without prompting "She's at Matt Gere's house in Portland "Jack had a small stifled giggle and said "She'll have him screaming by the end of the night,his head will be in his hands" "That is the truth cousin Jack" said Jim.

Ned brought down six open beers. Cousin Jack took a swig and masticated "What do you ask for if you are feeling really randy?" I don't know said Betsy Joe. "A pint of Jack spaniels and a falling fuck" declared cousin Jack with a flourish. Everyone started laughing.

Lou had a headache,she went down and faced the enemy. Gere said "You are married now Louise you must have liiiked Scotland theeen" McPhail who was fixing up another bowl of poison said "C'mon baby". "Yeah I love Scotland, the people there are the best race in the world" replied Lou

Jim said bravely to cousin Jack "I hear you had a little difficulties with one of your neighbors,-that she is sore with you" Jack grinned a 24 carat smile at Jim and replied "You don't feed off the kids Jim she is a crazy dog" BJ looked at Jack with rising excitement in the safety of Swiss Cottage, Jesus thought Jack looking back at BJ—what is that poor fat soul going to do when Ned and Jude die, join a convent?

"You have never fully read a book in your life McPhail" said Lou to the Willie Kaufman reading artist "Have you heard of James Joyce, Flannery O Brien or Franz Kafka-in Scotland I spent a year at an Adult college where the warden Edwin Muir the poet had been the first person to translate Kafka into

English IT was like Ruskin college Mannie-Newbattle"—Mannie Ruskin was another adult artist and educator that McPhail had never heard of and what's worse he didn't even care about the fly blown cemetery that was modern Europe.

Jack asked Jim if he was looking forward to going to Mexico, Jim said he was and the road trip would let him see a little of the West coast. "You're going to see it all Jim," said Jack. A police siren hooted far away and Ned suddenly said quickly "watch out in LA son." Jimmy pulled the comforter close to him,he was still keeping his chin above water and concentrated on the blue glare of the television show. It was "The Tonight" shows and Madonna and Rachel Weis were engaged in a little coffee talk.

Matt Gere said it was getting late McPhail was miffed and Said he had to go soon-he had an audition tomorrow for a commercial for Les Schwab tires. What was the point in saying anything thought Lou-what did these two Wasps know about Soweto or Stompe Maketze or Steve Biko. Gere said to McPhail "Go rad boy go" McPhail put on his Boss Jacket-the one his mother had bought for him and went to say goodbye to Lou. He said "bye Macleod" and Lou replied like a car flipping a bitch "Go rad boy go-on the other side bros" Gere saw McPhail to the door and his bucking Bronco.

Lou arrived back at Swiss Cottage about eleven-she stopped held the wheel for a few seconds and sighed in relief. Gere had tried it on with her but she was more than a match for him-she had slept on the couch and had slipped out unnoticed at 8am. Before hitting the freeway she had stopped at Winchells and got some coffee and chocolate dough ring in the dawning rimy cold. She said to herself "The fall and rise of a Scots American."

She went in-Jude was in the kitchen-Jude was reading a letter. She looked up with her glasses on and declared "Well hello there Mrs. Cumming" Lou said as a railroad siren hooted in the near distance "Hi Mom I'm home" "Did you get breakfast honey" said Jude concerned "I stopped at Winchells Mom" said Lou "Whats your letter about Mom?" "It's a letter from the hospital I have to go for a cat scan of my womb" "Oh Mom said Lou you're not sick are you?" "It's just a routine test on my medical insurance-nothing to worry about" Said Jude holding the letter to her left breast. Lou went and got some juice from the refrigerator and said I'm going to check on Jim the sleeping beauty. Jude put the letter down and said "You be gentle with Jim honey".

Jim had woken up when he heard his wife. Lou appeared in the doorway she had brought through some coffee for Jim-with half and half and white sugar. She sat on the edge of the double bed and said "Here Jim for you" Jim said "Thanks Lou" and he drank some Coffee and placed the cup on a Jim Beam coaster on the bedside cabinet.

Jim took Lou in his arms and kissed her wildly. Sunshine and a cool breeze blew in through the curtained window. Jim had a massive erection he was lying naked. Lou pulled down the comforter and started masturbating Jim's cock. She leant down and over Jim's cock and balls and continued to masturbate Jim. Lou could smell a slight odor of fish from Jim's glans penis and she began to suck him off. She then sucked his tight little ball sac and licked the back of his cock. She then took the whole of Jim's cock in her mouth and gave him deep throat in an experienced fashion. She then laid her head on Jim's thigh and continued to masturbate his large erect penis. His glans was purple and engorged with blood. Jim exclaimed "I'm coming Lou" and she quickly took the glans of his penis in her mouth. His white gissum came inside her mouth and he sighed in orgasmic relief as Lou held his balls in her hand. Lou tasted the fresh grass of his cum and swallowed. Jim then tenderly lifted Lou's head up to his head and held her gently for what seemed like an eternity. "I love you Jim my husband and protector," said Louise. "Aint nothing like the real thing Baby" said Jim with a smile on his face.

Jim rose from the bed and put on a fresh pair of jocks. He then lay upright on the bed and drank some more coffee. Lou laid her head on his bare chest and said "A penny for your thought Jim". Jim looked ahead and said "Cousin Jack was here for an hour last night". Lou said accentuating her soft French American accent "Was he . . . how was that porridge features" "He was talking about Banes and how he had dobbed her in" "That crazy little dog with her big bum honey-a new love correction" Jim put on the radio it was Womack and Womack with "Teardrops". "Cousin Jack once had a one night stand with her about twenty years ago" said Lou dreamily. She looked at her manicured nails-they would need buffing and filing tonight. "Do you think there will be trouble Lou? "If there is well that's alright with me Jim-you'd be surprised how far Cousin Jack reaches and how he can handle himself-Jack was quite a dude in his motorcycling days" Lou went and stood up, she said she was going for a crap and a shower and a change of fresh clothes. Her new white per uno panties were pretty bloody by now. Jim got dressed and went through to get some breakfast.

Jimmy was sitting there eating cheerios, -he was going back to LA on Boxing Day. He slurped the calcium,enriched milk in a disgusting fashion and looked up at Jim spluttering. Jude and Ned had gone down to the mall to shop for Christmas. Jude had left out some ubiquitous flat American sausage and eggs for Jim's breakfast. The skillet was on the hob.

Jim made his late breakfast quietly. Jimmy said to Jim "I smoke Rothmans Blue Jim are they cool in Europe?" "There is a fire at one end and a sucker at the other end in all fags Jimmy" Jimmy misunderstood what Jim had said and thought that Jim was insulting him. He replied to Jim "My my my said the spider to the fly step right ahead and you're dead"

LA was on the edge of the world, the Pacific Rim- where it took a long time for fashion to move to the left. For a city almost as large as Wales it was governed by stuffy conservative parochialism. Jim rose to his full 6' 2" and said to Jimmy "Whatever". He washed his plate, cup and cutlery and placed them on the draining board. He emptied the basin of soapy water with pouring satisfaction,for he was a water engineer, Jim looked out of the window and suddenly thought about George Lawrence the master drainer at Wimpeys. He had seen Dodd in Aberdeen divine water with two copper L shaped rods. George was one the finest men Jim had met in his life.

Louise came into the kitchen and said to Jimmy "We're coming to visit you Jimmy on the trip". "That will be a troublesome event Lou-you can ditch down in my dressing room" Jim sat down and folded his arms He thought about Lou lying on the floor in an airless dressing room struggling for breath. "At least we'll have a roof over our heads Louise It'll come as a welcome rest."

Jim was girding his loins for the trip in The New Years. He felt confident but there was all that trouble in LA-it would be a test that he would come through. Once the trip was over Lou and Jim are going to rent an apartment in Portland-the deposit money was going to be a late wedding present from Judith and Ned. They would have their freedom and their own place. It would be an exciting day.

Jimmy took a sip of his coffee and Lou sat down-she sucked up to her older adopted brother and said to Jimmy "How's the high flying oil business Jimmy?" "To be honest with you Lou I work hard and crunch numbers all day then come home and eat my dinner-The oil and gas industry sucks-I was good at Art at high school and I'm concerned that I will be made redundant"... "I really want to make it in the movies." Lou said gently. "We're all wannabes Jim but not everyone can be a film star." Vulnerable young self-pitying three year old thought Jim They don't know how lucky they are here.

Jimmy was a Matheson, he had been found on the steps of the Ventura Baptist church swaddled up with a nametag around his neck so Ned and Judith adopted him. Lou had told this to Jim back in Aberdeen. A North East name that in Scots language meant the maggots of the meat. A fighting clan of no clout whatsoever. What would Mannie Jim's father have said if he had married a Matheson for he believed in all that claptrap that there was a natural ascendancy in the world. Anyhow as it was the Macleods' and the Cummings' were both full clans in Scotland. It gave Lou and Jim both pointed intelligence if nothing else, an ability to assimilate the truth and deconstruct the Matheson's' of this world.

Jim said nothing for in truth he was a man of few words, he was a cowboy and that is beautiful. "It's Christmas," said Lou "A time for peace and understanding" for Jim could have championed Jimmy if he would let him.

Lou said "Jim and I are going to Grant Cumpstons tonight to pick up the tent for our trip to Mexico- you're welcome to ride with us if you want to Jimmy" Jimmy thought about it he had bought all his presents in LA he could use a change of scenery so he said "Yeah I'll tag along if that's alright with Jim" Jim said "Of course that's fine with me Jimmy, you know that" "Well that is decided then Jimmy we'll go down about eight in the Toyota".

Lou put her glass in the sink and shook her fingers dry of water. Then Jimmy and Lou went down to the den to watch the PAL TV. Jim went and stuck his ECOSSE sticker on the back of the Toyota. Jude and Ned arrived back as Jim was doing this and Jude said, "That'll attract some attention down in LA"

JACK NICHOLSON

They arrived at Grant's at the back of eight, it had been snowing slightly and Jim looked at the avenue of winter trees in outspread supplication. God how Jim and Lou hated the winter months for they both died a little bit each winter. The mild pacific winter was a novelty to Jimmy. Both he and Jim had both bought six bottles of full sail blue amber beer. And they went into the porch of the old slatted wooden property on Washington and Oklahoma. Richard Parker answered the door,-he was Grant's housemate. He was at U of O studying civil engineering and was an all star American Football player. Dick was a quarter back with pace and a v torso. Lou introduced Jimmy and Jim to Richard. Jimmy noticed Richard had a chisel chin that always needed shaving, get the barbasol out. Jim could tell that Richard was a splendid fellow. They all went into the living room MTV Oregon was on and Magenta Devine was interviewing the Cranberries. Lou pointed at the PAL TV and said "I remember once she was in The Satyricon and Matt Gere asked her to put her fist in her mouth and she tried it,fucking banger" Grant was in the kitchen and he shouted "HI". "Hi Hi" said Jimmy. Anna a Taiwanese girl was sitting on the couch,she was Dick's girlfriend and a nurse. She worked at the hospital and she was eating takeaway Chinese food chop suey. A guy was sitting watching the TV on the floor he stood up and introduced himself as Mannie Falconer. Everyone shook hands and sat down.

Lou went through to the kitchen with three bottles of full sail looking for the bottle opener. Grant was standing there looking at the Oregonian newspaper. He was chewing skol tobacco-Grant was originally from Kentucky and was in his final year at the U of

O. He was a black boy.

Grant said in perfunctory fashion "Hi Lou"
"Do you have a spare bottle opener Grant?" "Here let me Lou" and he pulled a bottle opener from his pocket on a chain that held his billfold. Grant opened the bottles. Grant was the lead guitarist and singer in a band called Gravel Pit. They had had some success and had recently cut a record in Portland. Grant's sense of humor was as dry as a post and he said to Lou "Where is your kilt?" Lou replied "Och aye; Donald where's your Troosers" "Awesome" replied Grant. The house smelt of fugue an American smell associated with these wooden houses.

Lou picked up the bottles and said "C'mon Grant grab your beer let's go and join the wildlife." They both went through to the living room. Dick was busy telling Jim about a game of rugby they had had with a select Scottish university rugby side recently in Eugene, "They wiped our asses, the Scots wiped the floor with us." Jim took his beer from Lou and said, "The Scots international side are absolutely massive. They train on porterhouse steak and pints of milk. My first girlfriend Nina is dating Mannie Beattie, he started out as a civil engineer but does radio work now" He's a lovely guy from Glasgow" Oh really said Dick "You've met Mannie Beattie!" "I was once staying in a hotel in Edinburgh in 1984 on a course with my employer Tarmac and I went down for my breakfast one morning with a hangover and the entire 1984 grand slam squad were sitting there eating their breakfast. Gavin and Scott Hastings Mannie Calder the whole squad grinned at me I had just been dumb mouthed, Mannie Jeffries booted the priceless Calcutta cup about the Scotland dressing room and put a pornographic magazine in my room the night before, just to suggest that there was the possibility of a sex life after that wee honey Nina, "Oh shut up Casanova" said Lou "You told me that you were miserable that summer you old drunk, you got done for drink driving at the end of that summer at the Braemar Gathering and lost your drivers license" "What's the Braemar Gathering Lou?" said Grant. Jim replied for her and said "It's caber tossing and bagpipe competitions, that sort of thing; The British Royal Family attend every year-Braemar is near Aberdeen" "Awesome" said Grant. "By all accounts the only thing you were tossing that summer was your weener" Said Lou. Everyone including Jim started laughing. They all thought it was terribly funny.

Mannie and Jimmy were both now sitting together on the couch. Mannie was gay and the lucky lad around town. He worked in a cycling shop as a mechanic. Jimmy was rolling up a joint with a job paper. Soon the marijuana was being passed around. "I know your father Ned," said Mannie "He's a good and noble man" Jimmy lied and said "He brought me up the right way" Jimmy and Mannie both fancied each other and Lou reckoned that Jimmy wouldn't be coming home with them tonight. Jimmy fancied a bag off.

Anna had been saying nothing, she was a thoughtful girl who didn't normally smoke pot, but she did on this occasion. It was Christmas. She worked in A&E and most of the injuries were ghastly gunshot and knife wounds. She and Dick really loved each other and they were planning on getting married once Dick was working as a civil engineer. Jim told Dick he had a degree in civil engineering-that he had a fair bit of experience as a site engineer. Dick said, "Civils on site in this country are known as surveyors; it's all about the final frontier here pal." Jim said he didn't know if he fancied working as a surveyor, he would have to re-train, as a surveyor for it was an entirely different system of setting out in this country. In a tic Lou reminded him that he wasn't just here to party, that he would have to find a job so he could take his place in the house of fun. "We get kicked out of home after high school in America Jim and have to fend for ourselves-everyone who is capable does something to survive," said Grant.

Jim quickly thought about BJ; poor bitch. Where was there common decency-the milk of human kindness. In America? He quickly snorted like a bull in rut. When he left high school he had just wanted to be a poet. He had written many bad verses His similes were hackneyed his metaphors lumpen and then he had said no more poems ,that's enough. Jim had a propensity to float though ,he had written the poems for Nina. He knew in his heart that he did deserve the title of poet not now perhaps maybe never.

Setting out was an art form ,there was nothing more beautiful than the three, dimensional parabolic curve set out in the clay soil. This was the mark of the true poet and now Jim felt ready to never return to the whack and clatter of the construction site. He looked down diffidently as he was wont to do and Lou put her arm around his shoulders spontaneously. She knew that Jim would find his métier here in America. The evidence was immutable.

Every American guy in the room was trying to out talk the other with loud conversation. They all suffered from Attention deficit hyperactivity disorder thought Jim. This made the old cowboy somber and he said nothing. This aspect of American life Jim found ghastly. On that note he decided to tell a joke or two. He said loudly "What do you call birds that drink too much, Toucans!" Everyone laughed loudly. Lou then told a joke. She startled giggling and said "Did you hear about the panda that went into a restaurant and shot the waiter? It was reported the next day, a panda eats shoots and leaves!" everyone laughed at that one as well. Jim then came back with "What does a mole use to dig holes in the garden with?" Everyone including Lou was mystified at that one. Jim declared "His spades!" That one didn't get so much of a laugh.

Jimmy and Mannie went through to the kitchen for some privacy, they had a lot of private jokes to share and Dick came and sat beside Anna. In the living room they all lit up cigarettes except Anna, she didn't smoke. The beers were going down smoothly—there was hope for everybody. Jimmy said to Mannie, "I have a present ready for you Mannie-I have a little black book in my room." Mannie said, "Where's the tee shirt?" Jimmy felt like pulling Mannie's pants down He was absolutely gagging for it. "We can make it happen later on," said Jimmy with a smirk. Mannie tried not to gloat and said, "We can laugh about it after that come on." "Hit it," said Jimmy and Mannie started kissing him wildly. Jimmy had got everything today.

Grant stood by the warm wood burning stove and stroked his beard thoughtfully,it was a moment of gentle repose. He said "Who is cooking tomorrow Lou?" Lou replied "Me of course,Jim will help me won't you Jim" "Whatever" said Jim wonderingly. "We're having some of the team over tomorrow I'll be cooking for five jocks" said Dick. Grant thought aloud and said "It will be awesome".

"It will be happening around 4PM," said Anna. Shirley Manson and Garbage came on MTV Oregon, she was originally from Edinburgh and had been in a band called Goodbye Mr. Mackenzie named after a brief affair with Connor. They had cracked America and Shirley was singing "Stupid Girl" Grant stared at the PAL TV and said, "She's mine". "Stink ah fish," said Jim in finest Doric. Lou and Anna started laughing.

This black musician won't turn down Shirley thought Grant. "Can you let us know when you get there?" said Lou. Grant hadn't kicked ass with a woman for almost ten years and he couldn't figure out what women were there for in the first place. Grant used to drink Knob Creek on his own sometimes and when he did this he turned into a vicious alcoholic.

Lou and Anna struck up a conversation
"I always admired your independence Lou
"Oh god yeah extremely"
"You should write a novel Louise"
"It'll be an extremely long speech"
"Dealing with deeper darker issues of Europe Lou"
"Yeah there all far more pretentious over there Anna"
"You would suit a beard Lou," said Jim
"What's next for you Anna?"
"A lion heart called Richard Lou"

Lou said, "We'll have to be going soon." Grant said, "I'll go and get the tent for your trip to Baha California Lou." Jim went and used the bathroom-he needed to pee, after he finished piddling he looked in the mirror and noticed he had a large in growing hair on the side of his chin. He found a rusty safety pin in the Toilet cabinet and dug the hair out. It bled a little but he didn't think anymore about it and went back downstairs. Grant had come through with the tent and said it was a two-person tent that you could put up inside as well as on the beach.

Calum Cumming

CHAPTER SIX

Jimmy arrived at Swiss Cottage at around eleven am with his golden wave still just about intact. It was a clear bright day and the sun shone through the timberline. A small plane droned high up in the sky. Jimmy wished he could stay for good. He went in to the kitchen and said happy Christmas Mom, happy Christmas Lou. It was Thursday. Lou looked at him with a smile and said, "Better to be hung for a sheep rather than a lamb." Jim was sitting at the table peeling potatoes. The Turkey was in the oven. Jim had stuffed the cavity with oatmeal, onion and olive oil stuffing.

Lou had been up since six, she had made a Christmas cake. She had sifted the flour and mixed spice into a large mixing bowl. She added 1Lb of self raising flour, two teaspoons of mixed spice, 8 oz of castor sugar, 6 oz currants, 6 oz of sultanas, 4oz fresh stoned cherries, 4 large eggs, 4 tablespoons of milk and 8 tablespoons of brandy. Lou sliced up margarine. She had mixed thoroughly then beat with a wooden spoon for one minute.

Lou had spooned into a greased and lined 8-inch round deep cake tin. She had placed the cake into the center of a slow oven (333 degrees F) and baked for one and a half hours then lowered the heat to cool (310 degrees F) and baked for a further hour. Lou had pushed a warm skewer gently into the center of the cake, and it had come out a clean stick. She was allowing the cake to cool before removing it expertly from the tin.

Jimmy said he was off for a shower and a shave-he disappeared downstairs with a Christmas pie to rest his bottom. In a tic BJ came into the kitchen for her morning meds. She reached deep in the cupboard. Jim felt a little paranoid it was the first time he had spent a Christmas away from his mum and his brother Mannie Patrick. Was his Christmas about to be confirmed by history?

Ned was away hitting balls on Christmas morning with his partner Chuck Eagleburger. Although the old tiger was limping, he had dropped the frozen turkey on his left foot the previous night. Jude was taking photos with her Kodak instamatic and she took one of Lou and Jim-Lou's face was smudged with flour. This had never been captured by camera in quite the same way.

BJ didn't like her photo being taken although she posed with Jim and Jude. "C'mon BJ" said Lou. Lou repeated the public shot for that which sent shivers up BJs' spine did not inform Lou's natural opinion. She said, "Wake up BJ it's a beautiful morning"

Lou sat down and drank her coffee. She said, "Israel is at war with Palestine since the 1920s and here we are celebrating Christ's birth-the holy paradigm." Jim had finished peeling the potatoes and said to Lou, "Ecclesiastes is the opposite of fortune cookie where everything is going to turn out fine."

Jude said, "So you've read your bible then Jim." "I

have read most of the new testament and some of the Old Testament. The Jews have offended by killing Jesus Christ with the Romans acquiescence. Lenny Bruce said we killed Christ for three days only I enjoyed my streaky bacon for breakfast." Lou started laughing and said, "Crispy in the oven". Jude came back with, "Just like the turkey.I'll go and baste it." Jim took a drink of his coffee and said "At the heart of the celebration is the Jews remembrance of what happened to them in the Holocaust. The story is much richer than the current middle eastern conflict."

"It certainly makes a great bit of television Jim," Said Jude who was peeping into the oven. "There but for the grace of god go I," said Lou. "The military leaders of the Arabs think that they are cousins of the Zionists," said Jim. "Do not do unto to others what is hateful to you," said Jude. "Well try and have cousin Jack done for dealing fucking drugs then Mom, you wont get very far!" "Cousin Jack is a hero," said Jim. "You don't make sense honey, but I agree Cousin Jack is an old geezer who has had a good life-condition soul." Said Judith who was now basting the fowl.

"Cousin Jack is coming over tonight after dinner so we can look forward to that," said Jude. Lou and Jim said they were going for a walk.Lou had to cool off. She went and got her beat jacket. Jim put on his wine red Levi. They left the house walked down to the T-junction and took a right past the end of the asphalt and into the woods. It wasn't very safe in the woods as there were timberline wolves in there.

Lou walked ahead fearless-she found a stick to

guide her, a walking pole. Jim sparked up an old gold took a couple of draws and passed the cigarette to his wife who had now slowed down to walking pace on the track beside her husband. She was glad to be in the company of this fantastic guest on Christmas day. "Can I put a call through to my mum Betsy tonight Lou?" "Sure honey" said Lou. "She must be wondering about you by now" "I'll call about eight then" "Sure Honey," said Lou. They walked on gossiping.

Jim wooed her for Lou's heart needed building up after Jude's comment about Cousin Jack. "How is it that a man loves a treacle pudding Lou."? "I don't know how does he," said Lou who was giggling now. "He chases her around the forest with a wooden spoon." "Are you going to spank my bum Jim please do". . . Jim caressed her right bottom cheek and gave it a little squeeze.

Jim put his arm around Lou who was very supple in his arms. He kissed her on the mouth and mimed, "I will never ever let you go." Lou broke apart and said, "Where are the sweets you promised me?" Jim said in a mock American voice, "It just so happens I have a packet of rolos in my Levi pocket" Lou said "Please Jim," like a little babe and Jim gave her one. He felt like riddling her in the wood but it was hoary and cold. He said, "What Heats the beat throbs the knob that dangles the angle." "My period is got over by now Jim". . .

They walked on to a clearing that was fenced off from the dark wood. They linked arms. A small dappled roe deer was eating grass through the fence. It was startled but surprisingly did not run off but continued to eat the lush grass. Jim started mouthing, "Cheep cheep" and the deer rose it's head and looked at them. "It's a male you can see his buds," said Jim. "He's beautiful Jim," said Lou in wonder. "C'mon" said Jim, "Let's leave him to croon." They walked on the path and continued to gossip. Lou said, "Lets go to cougar dam tomorrow Jim it's a hot spa. It's great up there above the timberline in the Cascades." "I'm up for that," said Jim the willing victim. Little did he know?

They walked further on and almost were back on the private estate. They had walked a half circle. They suddenly heard a wolf howl-it was blood curdling. The dog wasn't far off and Lou said to Jim, "C'mon lets hurry on down to Swiss cottage." Jim said, "Hallelujah they are scared of humans." "They are so intelligent Jim," said Lou as they walked slowly in the veneer of the estate. Classical Civilization. They went into Swiss cottage and Lou shouted, "Mom I'm home." Jude was setting the table in the open plan dining room that lay at the rear of the upstairs lounge. Jim went and had a pee in the bathroom, the coffee and the cold acted like a diuretic on his bladder. He had drunk a lot of beer last night but he was feeling fine today. Jimmy was grooming the golden wave in the den. He had showered and shaved and had put on fresh clothes. Sitting on his lap was Jim's present that was a Romeo Y Juliet large Havana cigar. He was wrapping it in Christmas paper that he had got from his Mom.

Jim came and sat on the couch and looked at the PALTV. It was The Streets Of San-Francisco with Karl Malden and a young Michael Douglas. He looked at schnozzle puss Karl Malden and thought about the man in Aberdeen who was known as cancer beak,he had a massive tumor on his nose and lived beside The Grammar School in Easement Avenue. It was almost as disfiguring as a wine stain. Jim looked at Jimmy; little did he know . . . Jim said to Jimmy, "Are you going to see Mannie again." Jimmy replied "Without love we are like ships in the night." Well that decides that thought Jim. Jim went upstairs to Lou in the bedroom. She was changing into her kilt. She had brushed her clean hair and it hung like sea snakes on her haunting shoulders. Take a look up the rail track from Miami to Canada. Linwood no more, Lochaber no more, Lewis no more, Skye no more, Sutherland no more. Bathgate no more, Irvine no more, Methyl no more. No more violence.

Jim said to Lou honestly, "Life was a small delay without you." Lou replied, "Do you like me in my kiltie?" Jim started laughing and said, "My eyes are popping out of my head!" How could Jim resist the aroma of Lou's scent? It had started with a kiss. The distant look in Lou's eyes.

Ned was back from the range and was limping slightly. He sat briefly with Chuck Eagleburger in the kitchen. Chuck was smoking a mild seven cigar. He said, "How's the limey shaping up, are you going to take him down to the bleachers and the U of O basketball?" "Jim prefers soccer," replied Ned. "Same rules more or less he'll come round," said Chuck. "He's doing great" said Ned. "He's going to shout it to the top," said Ned. "That's great," said Chuck. "For Scotchmen don't lack spunk." Chuck went out the front door after wishing Judith a happy Christmas. He had said to her, "Home again to

Martha Judith."

Lou had on a black Playtex bra and wore a white cotton shirt. She squirted on some Miss Dior perfume. She put on her comfortable black Chinese slippers to her size 5 feet. Louise put in her gold opal ear studs and put on her silver name bracelet. Like Morrissey's one.

Lou turned on the radio, it was Van Morrison, the bright side of the road. Lou started singing. Jim had gone to get a shave and change his shirt.

While Jim was in the bathroom Louise wrapped Jim's present-it was Abroad in America edited by Robert Blow. She had ordered and bought the book in Mannie Smiths in Glasgow. Lou inscribed the book, "For my loving husband Jim Robert Macleod Cumming on his arrival in the New World Christmas day 1992."

They ate at 5pm. Jim and Jimmy and Ned had happily coexisted in the Den from around four. Over Buds the conversation had ranged widely from the latest weather to the news on TV. Jimmy said to Ned "I think I am going to move to Oregon Pa-The Oregonians are fantastic they make money from everything." Ned replied in his slow Albany drawl, "There's not so much goddam shit up here Jimmy". "I really like the men in Eugene". Said Jimmy. "Perhaps you are experiencing a crisis", said Ned. He understood Jimmy not being content with being a clay baker, he was immoral as well. "Grant moved heere from Kentucky-I meht hiim last night he's maade it" said Jimmy weakly. "Grant is an artist Jimmy you're just a late addition to the party". Said

Jim cruelly but brutally honestly.

Jimmy was just concerned with himself, he was like the president of the board on the gurney. Jimmy was a damned soul, the bare facts suggested that he was destined to reach the end of the road fitting into 20th century western thought-a lonely old man. The golden wave wouldn't last forever.

BJ had been in her room watching Angels with dirty faces with James Cagney. She lived in an assisted fantasy world. Perhaps the voluntary job with the Red Cross would broaden her horizons beyond the loneliness of Generation-X. She was on the cusp of perhaps replacing, that which was obsolete in her life with something new.

Lou came downstairs with a glass of Napa red and lifted the tone. She said aloud, "You're looking dandy Jimmy ready to fall in love with the fun Lovin' criminals" Jimmy replied, "The divine status of the artist is lost to me since I had my mucky paws on David Hackney"... Jim laughed ho ho. Coarse Caledonian tinkers thought Lou. She said to Ned "I hope you're hungry pops I made grits especially for you." Ned replied in his slow Schenectady drawl, "You know I like my grits honey" He was looking at Lou's legs and could only imagine Lou's mojo. Jim caught him staring and he thought you old pervert. Lou broke it down and said, "If you don't see it then you don't believe it".

LL sat down on the L shaped casting couch. She took a drink of her wine and said, "Is Betsy Joe going to come out of her room. Jimmy shouted "BJ" and she opened the door a crack and stuck her nose out. As if sniffing the air. Lou said, "C'mon BJ when was the last time you hugged your Pa".

> Our Father in Heaven
> Hallowed be your name
> Your True Kingdom comes
> You will be done
> On earth as it is
> In Heaven
> Give us this day
> Our daily bread
> And forgive us
> Our debts
> As we also have
> Forgiven our
> Debtors
> And lead us not
> Into temptation
> But deliver us
> From evil

"Amen," said Lou. She had delivered the Lord's Prayer and now they tucked in to smoked salmon, salted butter, rye bread and lemon. Ned sat at the head of the table facing Judith. On his right sat Jim, on his left BJ. On Jude's left sat Lou, on her right Jimmy. "This is great fish," said Ned milling some black pepper and squeezing lemon juice on to his smoked salmon. "It's sockeye," said Lou breezily. The fish had been Jim's suggestion. A European contribution. Jim could eat smoked salmon until he was blue in the face.

Pretty soon they had tasted the last of the fish and Jude took the empty plate through to the kitchen.

Lou went to help her mother with the turkey. Jim topped everyone's glass up with Napa red. Jim said to Ned, "I wouldn't mind selling some ping irons in Scotland.I could make a fortune, you could get BJ to bring some over." "I don't think that would be a very good idea", said Ned protectively in his slow Albany drawl. Old cunt thought Jim,no sense of entrepreneurship. Ned spoke and said, "Neither I nor Jude intend to make no further comment on your money making scheme Jim I regard your comment as a closed chapter".

BJ was in a heated discussion with Jimmy,the golden wave shone brightly under the candlelight. They were talking about the star Robert Redford. BJ said, "He was a great actor until his face turned to leather". Old boot thought Jimmy he had always fancied Robert Redford for that blue-eyed boy truly did have a golden wave. Jimmy left BJ sitting like a lemon and said, "He is beautiful he has started a second career at the rainbow of Sundance and he moisturizes with T gel the old cat wears it" "I suppose he's not gay Jimmy" said BJ coming back with a body shot out of the blue. "And he won the Oscar for directing "Ordinary People" said Jimmy.

"Now now Children," said Schnozzle puss, "No bickering at the Christmas table." Jude brought through the turkey on the ashet for Ned to carve. Then Jude took the dinner plates out of the oven where they were warming. They were having broccoli, carrots and peas and Brussels sprouts. Lou had made the gravy with corn flour paste and a chicken stock cube. She brought through the mash and the roast potatoes. She then brought through the grits, the gravy and the plates. Jim opened a new bottle of

Napa red and placed the open bottle on the table. He sat back down. Ned stood up and began carving the 14Lb bomb with his electric Kenwood carver. It gave off a zizzing noise as he carved the large bird.

Jim was reminded of a kebab shop he had gone into with Connor back in Aberdeen. The Turk's electric carver had given off the same zizzing noise and a man with ankle black and white cowboy booties had come into the shop looking like Bob Dylan on ecstasy. They had both looked at each other and burst out laughing. The zizzing noise continued and Lou and Jim burst out laughing.

They all helped themselves to vegetables and gravy and settled down to eat the feast.

"You cowboy," said Jimmy "This is good turkey". He had broken the sound of silence and the conversation turned to Kuwait and operation Desert Storm. The allies had liberated Kuwait but had not gone after Saddam the old Taurean. Jim looked down at his plate. "The Iraqi army was left sucking diesel they were all burnt to a cinder". "The allies certainly took back the night," said Lou," helping herself to more broccoli-she loved broccoli.

Everyone had a glass of water and a bread roll at their side and Jim said "Adam's brew.The wars of the 21st Century are going to be fought over water. The world population is unsustainable. In the Middle East potable water is more valuable than gold-the water of this world neither decreases or increases it is an unsustainable natural resource in the face of population explosion. Economics teaches you that". Jim said, "Cheers," and drank some USA Oregon water.

"We're going up to Cougar Dam hot springs tomorrow Mom" said Lou. BJ started laughing and said, "Helter Swelter". Jim looked at her quizzically. "Cougar springs sure beats new layout junctions for Eugene," said Ned slyly.

They all pulled some crackers and everyone was crowned with a paper hat. It was a chance to express them and they had been given the nighttime edit. Lou looked sexy and speechless in her green paper hat,it went with her eyes-blue green lake Windermere in Cumbria.

Jim helped himself to some cranberry sauce and let it linger on the teaspoon. Pretty soon everyone had finished their plate and their stomachs were groaning. Jude asked Jimmy if he wanted some more turkey. He replied, "I'm stuffed Mom." Lou and Jim cleared the table to make way for the plum duff and custard. Lou said to Jim in the kitchen, "We carry brandy on this galleon". She poured a liberal tot of brandy on the duff lit it and carried it through to the dining room. Jim could hear from the kitchen where he was jugging the custard Jude exclaim dirtily, "Ooh La La quell surprise."

They sat down and ate their plum duff and custard. Jim thought I'm going to give Louise one up the duff later tonight. She was gagging for it thought Jim.

The pudding was soon over and Lou and Jude cleared the table. It had been coffee and Christmas cake with a Drambuie follow an excellent Christmas dinner,to. They all opened their Christmas presents, which had been under the tree in the lounge. Jude and Ned had given Jim an LLBean golf jacket,it was all shiny blue and new. Jim tried it on-it fitted perfectly.

They all sat down for Drambuie in the Den except BJ who retreated to her room. Jim was smoking his Romeo Y Juliet cigar for he carried a cigar clipper. He said to Ned "A woman's a woman but a cigar is a good smoke". He put on a tape,it was The Gypsy Kings-passionate Spanish music about love and loss.

"This Spanish music,George Orwell fought in The Spanish Civil War and was invalided out,he was shot in the throat by General Franco's fascists," said Jim generally. "Have you read him Ned his work stays with you a whole while longer? He died of Tuberculosis before his three score and ten was up." Ned said "I've seen the film 1984.It's a totalitarian view of hell on earth where Big Brother Richard Burton watches everything you do,it must be like that in Iraq." Jim replied loudly "Don't confuse Liberty with freedom-Democracy is out of style. The alternative to Saddam is even worse that that monster drawing circles in the sand with his forefinger. "George Bush is a fucking war hero but a cunt with it." Said Lou absently.

Lou was looking girlishly at the assortment of down town Calvin Klein panties that her parents had bought her for Christmas,she always needed new panties. She took a wee belt of her brandy and was content with her VSOP digestive. Jude had started reading her book The First Man-it was an existential allegory that condemned the Soviet communism, the

Gulag and Stalin's totalitarianism. It was written in the belief that ideology must serve humanity not the contrary,although Camus was a deeply flawed man who betrayed his wife with other women many times in the course of their marriage.

Jimmy had got $100 dollars for his Christmas and he was content with that,it kept his empty billfold company. Lou sait to cher noter in French, "Il est un terrain de jeux maman» «OUI mon» cher repli Jude

Jim asked Jude if he could put a call through to his mother in Stafford Street in Aberdeen and she replied, "Yes please do, you go as well Louise and speak to Betsy." Lou and Jim went upstairs to Jude's study and placed a call long-distance.

Betsy answered the phone and Jim spoke to his mother.

"Hello Mum Happy Christmas its Jim"

"Hello darling it's five in the morning here, Happy Christmas, I was wondering when you were going to phone-are you settling in okay?"
"Yeah-everything's fine,I has met a lot of Lou's friends and family. I'm at Ned and Judith's it's nine pm here."
"It will soon be time for breakfast"
"We ate at 5pm we had turkey and trimmings"
"Lovely darling, we're had duck, Mannie Patrick made it. Bruce came round"
"Larry Grayson boy,the eternally depressed bowtie bachelor"
"Yes that's exactly right darling"
"Are you aye kicking the leggiest then-in a dirl oh

dubs"?

"What else de yeah expect from a bull's arse but shite Jim"

"Only joking mum is Mannie Patrick well?"

"The common weel darling"

"Has he found a job yet or is he still the trivia master of Scotland-playing those bloody machines in pubs!"

"He makes a living from it Jim-he'll find himself."

"I'm going to put you on to Lou she's dying to speak to you"

Jim handed the phone to Louise who had been sitting crossing and uncrossing her lovely legs. Jim could only imagine. . .

"Hello Bets Fit likes, sorry to phone so early"

"That's alright,it's wonderful to hear your voice-doos are aye picking Lou-happy Christmas darling!"

"Happy Christmas Betsy-Lang may your lum Reek"

"Are you happy to be home with your ain people?"

"I miss you Mum and George the cat"

"We both miss you around here Jim, but it's not forever.

"NO definitely not"

"Is Scotland just a parochial little country then compared to America?"

"No I certainly wouldn't say that, Scots people are loved where ever we go in this slick world"

"Did you miss the Queen's speech in America Jim?"

"I don't think so somehow"

"Oh be quiet Jim she does a wonderful job the old ducky"

"Yes all in all I'm forced to agree with you she's a wonderful ambassador"

"Scotland is a special country mum but there is so much pain there that I'm glad to be free of it at the

moment"
"I hope you find a job alright Jim there is a big recession starting here,it's tough to find a job even in Aberdeen."
"Something will turn up"
"You haven't lost your optimism Jim"
"No Mum I really love my wife"
"Cherish that love and watch it grow Jim"
"Okay mum I'll make you proud of me.Lisa and I"
"Goodbye Jim kiss kiss"
"Bye Mum"

Jim put the phone down and reflected for a minute about the auld country before he went back downstairs to the party. He thought Aberdeen; dirty old town, but he still had a sentimental attachment to that hard fishing port. He stood up and thought would he lose that attachment when his mother died?

Jim went downstairs to the den and took his seat on the casting couch. Lou said to him, "Are you sad my love?" Jim started laughing and suddenly thought about Morrissey-He looked at Lou's bracelet and replied, "Are you sad my Dr. Strangelove," Lou came back with a Texan drawl and shouted from the back of her throat, "Ride me cowboy."

Cousin Jack arrived around nine-he glided down the stairs like smoke through a keyhole. He had brought with him a bottle of chilled Lanson black label champagne with him. Jude went and got some glasses. Cousin Jack liked to just live. He was either an idiot or a genius.

Jack sat down he was wearing nice clothes. He had

on a navy blue, Mannieson Mills, single-breasted lambs wool jacket with a white soft cotton shirt and jazzy blue and yellow silk tie. He had on white chinos with black brogues. He smelt of expensive after shave and was smoking a Havana cigar.

BJ came out of her room because she loved Cousin Jack. BJ had never admitted to anyone except Jack that she suffered from mental illness. He gave her a reason to carry on. He was her foster uncle. He was the glue that held every social situation together.

Jude came down with the glasses and Jack raged against the boredom and popped the champagne cork-everyone had a glassful. Jack said, "Here is mud in your eye, Merry Christmas." Everyone wished him a Merry Christmas.

Lou went and put on another tape she had brought with her from Scotland-it was Duke Ellington live in Mexico. Very topical no?

Jack grinned his 24, carat smile at Lou and said, "Have you heard the joke about the Chinese team that went to the soccer World Cup." No I haven't," said Lou. Jack came out with the punch line, "They took a corner and opened a store." Everyone started laughing at that one. Lou said back to Jack, "How does Bob Marley like his doughnuts-With Jamming." Cousin Jack burst out laughing and grinned widely.

"Where did you have your Christmas dinner Cousin Jack?" Said BJ.
"I had it with Clay and Vickie Lindsay at my place. We had a substantial feast of goose in the High Street café." "Does Vicky still have her Busby

hairstyle," said BJ. "No it's primped pretty crubsy these days-wild stator and coconut oil." Replied Jack.

Louise punctured the safety of Christmas Day bubble of harmony, peace and safety and said to Cousin Jack, "Charles Prempeh told me about Carla Banes." "That little papist puppet with her sniggle teeth and bumble bee," said Jack. "I got a death threat in the mail on Tuesday, the picture of a dog and the message "I kill you." "So the case against Ms Chic is growing stronger by the day." said Lou. Jimmy, Ned and Jude had grown used to Cousin Jack's scrapes,this wasn't anything new to them.

"You don't deal drugs and feed off the kids, this is a brand new love correction." Said Jack tapping some ash into the tray. "Are you going to go to the cops Jack-about the death threat?" Said Lou. "Nothing new to the fuzz, just another grumpy story." said Cousin Jack suddenly hostile. "Banes isn't exactly a mountain in the world set of affairs,under the weight of her bed is the pounded skeleton in the cupboard." Said Cousin Jack. "Even so Jack the great slime kings are gathered in Portland for revenge." Said Jim draining his glass.
Jack replied, "I always take funerals in my stride Jim."

"That's the spirit," said BJ. "They don't call you the yellow jacket for nothing, it's the color of war Jack." "Excuse my language BJ but you can fuck the Pope and the IRA-I was born into the Pentecostal church and I look forward to the warm orange comfort of the harvest at the beginning of every September."

JACK NICHOLSON

Jimmy who had been saying nothing suddenly said, "Ho hum, you can't help being so machismo Cousin Jack-if only I really knew the truth like you." Lou said, "Och aye if you're a good wee boy I might give you a kiss Jimmy."

Jude and Ned said they were off too bed, early to bed early to rise, it was past 11. They wished Cousin Jack a goodnight and Jude gave him a cuddle and a kiss. Ned shook his hand warmly. Once they had departed the scene-exit stage right Jim told everyone a dirty joke. He said, "Did you hear about the dwarf who walked under a naked woman's legs- He got a crack on his head." Everyone guffawed loudly. Lou said to Cousin Jack "It's been a hard days night Jack when are we going to meet Jacqueline.The new Camelot!" Jack said deep in chest and gruffly, "I'm working on the case. She's got a lot of secrets to tell"... "You love her Jack,all the beauties in Scotland are from Scum Dee." Either Dundee or the Islands," said Cousin Jack. "As you know Lou our Macleods of Texas were originally from The Isle of Lewis in Scotland but they had shapely ankles,all that American breeding and good food." Said Cousin Jack.

The champagne was finished and everyone was rubicund and rosy. Jack lit a fresh old gold and said, "I had better be going-if you need me I'll be around. I'm going Nordic skiing up Mount Hood tomorrow but I'll be back on Saturday." "Okay Jack," said Lou who was still wearing her hat. Everyone embraced and shook hands and Lou and Jim saw Cousin Jack to the front door where the mistletoe was hanging from the ceiling. Lou kissed Jack on the lips and said, "Love you Cousin Jack." "I love you LL," said Jack.

Then he was gone in his black Cadillac.

Jim held Lou in his arms and said, "Have I the right to thrill you Louise?" "Kiss me," said Lou and Jim hugged his wife and kissed her. "Happy Christmas Louise." They trailed off to the bedroom. Lou shut the door, turned on the bedside light and kicked off her Chinese slippers. Jim sat her on the bed unbuttoned her blouse and took it off. He kissed her chest tenderly. He then unhooked her black bra and took it off. Lous nipples were huge and Jim suckled her for a few seconds holding her breasts. Lou's nipples were purple brown and Jim was turned on by the feint smell of sweat from Lou's shaved armpits. He then took off his shirt shoes socks and pants-he had a huge erection and he pulled back the foreskin and presented his faintly fishy penis to Lou to suck. He gently teased his wife and withheld his cock from being sucked. Just a little. Lou massaged his scrotum with her hand so his erection grew larger.

Jim undid his wife's kilt and took it off.she wriggled out of it with her sexy legs. He flung it on the chair. Jim felt thunder in his heart that he couldn't control. He looked at his wife's beautiful vagina trapped in her white per uno panties. He touched her clitoris underneath the cotton and Lou said "Take me baby I'm all yours." Jim pulled down her panties and smelled them,they smelt of vagina-a dark musky smell. He then gently spread his wife's legs and bent over her and masturbated her wet vagina with one hand, which he intermittently took to his wife's mouth where she sucked his fingers in pleasure. Lou said, "Let me mount you Jim." He lay on the bed and she straddled him guiding his erect penis into her wet vagina. She then rode him up and down. Jim kneaded her breasts and suckled her wonderful nipples. Then they kissed each other slowly at first but with growing passion as Lou began to climax. She moaned from deep in her throat. Jim held her tightly and put both his arms around her as his wife climaxed. She moaned in pleasure. She then dismounted from Jim and took the sixty-nine position with the sexual hot water bottle of her beautiful vagina and ass over Jim's hungry mouth. Jim ate her out, licked her clitoris and stroked the clean little rose of her ass. Lou was over her head with pleasure, it sure felt nice. Jim then roughly threw his wife on the bed and resumed the missionary position. The air was fragrant with the musky smell of Lou's moistly wet vagina. Jim rode her rhythmically until his wife climaxed again in body shuddering orgasm. They were both moist with sweat. Jim then came inside his wife his hot seed spreading into her uterus. They both lay exhausted.

CHAPTER SEVEN

Everyone was up early the next day. Jimmy was leaving for LA. They all said Goodbye to him and he took off-he was staying the night in San Jose near Frisco. Lou had said to him she would see him in the New Year on The Trip.

Jim and Lou got ready for their trip to Cougar Dam Hot Springs. Lou wore her white bikini under her clothes. They took off at ten and filled the car up with gas at the filling station at the supermarket at the bottom of the hill. Lou drove North East of Eugene for about an hour on 1-5 and turned east onto route 126. They then drove 7 miles up route 126 and turned left onto Main Street. And drove to the Cougar reservoir turnoff onto forest road 19 and drove 39 miles. Between mileposts 45 and 46 they turned right and drove to the Hydroelectric dam for 3 miles. Lou told Jim it trapped the water from the Mackenzie River, which was a tributary of the Willamette. Jim was fascinated by the perfect curve of the dam it was as beautiful as Ben Cruachan in Argyll shire back in Scotland. They turned right at the dam and went round the west side of the reservoir to the parking lot near the hot springs. They then walked 4 miles on the trailhead to the hot springs.

They held hands on their walk through the timberline and talked. Lou said, "I wonder if the springs have changed since I knew them? I used to come up here with some of the crowd from U of O and smoke pot and drink beer." In a tic Jim replied, "I suppose they have gone downhill like everything else in this world." Lou replied, "Given the right circumstances things can get better." "I'm sorry Lou" said Jim, "I didn't mean to sound cynical." "I like things to be simple clean and attractive Jim as you well know." Said Lou. Jim said, "I know darling hold me."

They embraced on the trailhead and Jim fondled his wife's breasts. He loved her so much.

In about an hour they arrived at the Hot Springs. There was a couple bathing in the springs they had no clothes on. "Do you promise to be a good boy Jim," said Lou. "Of course I will," replied Jim. They undressed in the open changing room and Jim was soon naked. Lou took all he had to offer here on Magic Mountain. Lisa brought the towel and some soap she had brought with her-for she hadn't had a shower that morning.

They both walked down the decking and slipped into the hot springs by the boulder head. The couple introduced themselves. "Hi I'm Todd and this is my wife Alanna." They were old hippies from Eugene. The steaming water was just the right temperature for it was chilly up there. They both sat on the rock ledge that was submerged. Lou decided to soap herself. Alanna was pretty tidy and Jim looked at her breasts momentarily. Lou washed her armpits and her breasts. She then took some soap and cleaned her bottom and her vagina. She passed Jim the soap and he cleaned himself including his penis and balls. He cleaned his bottom and armpits. He soaped his chest and submerged himself under the warm water. They were clean.

Todd said to Jim, "Sure is a nice day,sunny but cold partner." "Yeah," said Jim "We drove up from Eugene this morning." "Oh really you live in Eugene, I love your accent are you Irish?" Jim replied cool as a cucumber "No I'm Scots." Alanna had borrowed Lou's soap and was washing herself in the mid-day sun. Todd had a generous rug of chest hair. He must have been about 65 and looked like Willie Nelson. "The Scots are the true black men of Europe I'd love to visit your country if we ever make it to Europe." Said Todd. "My wife Lou here is American and I'm Jim; Jim Cumming."

Todd took his hand and said, "It's a real pleasure to meet you folks nice to make your acquaintance." "Likewise," said Lou. Alanna said to Lou "Did you have a nice Christmas," Yeah it was great," said Lou "We're staying with my parents just now in Eugene. We're moving to Portland in the New Year." "We're glad of your company here today," said Lou to Todd.

Carla woke up around twelve in her apartment on North East and Powell,she had a hash hangover. She took off her Pajamas and pulled on a new pair of panties. She had to lose some weight; she thought her ass was enormous. She momentarily looked at the black golden swirl of her pudenda and realized she still had it," I'm only 55 she said to herself". Carla skinned up a joint; she had got some hash oil last night and she decided to smoke the last of it before facing her day. Her pet Chihuahua Lady needed fed and she went into the kitchen to get some dog food and her plate. Billy Patterson her "business" partner had been over last night for his

Christmas dinner and he had used his hands to put the chicken on the plates. Even Carla had baulked at that. She fed the dog and smoked the joint leisurely. She put on her care worn dressing gown that was spattered with hash bombers. She realized her gap was tired she hadn't had a shower for a day. She would shower first thing this afternoon. She made herself some strong hot Lipton's tea and put milk and two white sugars in it. She went back into the bedroom and looked into the mirror. She had crow's feet coming from her eyes towards her brows and there were two deep furrows running down the sides of her nose. But she still had beautiful blue gray eyes. She had seen some amount of depravity in her short life.

"This is a nightmare," she said to herself. Carla was responsible for her own demise for she had tried every drug known to man and more than a little rose wine. There wasn't much to crow about she thought. She turned on the radio to a pop music channel for Carla loved pop music it was balm to her soul. Before she got caught up in drug dealing she had been a presenter for MTV Oregon. That was where she had met Cousin Jack in Corvallis Art School on a launch for Courtney Love's Hole. She looked in the mirror again at her caste Otto Dix face and thought aloud, "It could have been me I was a contender." That was before she lost her job for getting done drink driving on a rap in Portland one long hot weekend back in 1972. She had slammed the female officer in the face and spent the weekend in the county Jail. Not only did Carla lose her Drivers License but she lost her job as well.

That is when Carla had turned to drug dealing she

had started at first with marijuana but soon turned to class A drugs. Cocaine and pills. That is where the real money was to be found. She bought the drugs in bulk down in California and Billy and his underling Dike Harrower did the dirty stuff for her. It was perfect she thought she couldn't be caught. Very soon Carla was the biggest ecstasy dealer in Oregon and she couldn't get out of it even if she tried. She thought about Cousin Jack how he had been staying in her apartment back in 1974 before he had made it and she had shit on him. While he was trying to make it as a poet she had been shifting $30,000 of drugs a month and he was living on benefits of $18 a week. He even paid her rent for her when he lived in her apartment and she had the nerve to turn up every couple of weeks dealing drugs.

Well they say what goes around comes around and that is why Jack had turned her in when he saw an advertisement for the DEA in Eugene some 14 years later. For Cousin Jack was ruthless having been sent into a mental hospital by his girlfriend Ruth when he was staying at Carla's apartment. Her mother who had effectively ended the relationship died four years later of ovarian cancer. It's a tangled web we weave.

Carla didn't know it but she had lung cancer, She had been coughing blood up for a couple of weeks. On account of her 40 a day Marlboro Red habit. She had been smoking since she was 12.

Everyone had finished washing and Todd offered Jim one of his Luckiest. They both sparked up took a couple of draws and gave the cigarettes to their girls.

Todd said to Lou, "The sun fairly stole from my heart today mama". "We're in the most beautiful spot in Oregon," said Alanna. "Sure beats Aberdeen in Scotland," said Jim. "What do you do Todd. "I'm a poet and artist I work with Ken Kesey in U of O. Have you met Ken said Lou astonished. "Hell yeah," said Todd, "He's a hero of mine. He's not very well I'm afraid he had a liver transplant recently. The magic bus is in the garden of his homestead" Both Lou and Jim had read One Flew Over The Cuckoo's Nest and Lou had read the more difficult Sometimes A Great Notion. Kesey had known Neal Cassidy before he drank himself to death. It looked as though Kesey had gone down the same route. "Kesey was part of the beatnik counterculture of the 60s' but they paid the price for a shudder in the loins so to speak" said Todd. "There are none of us granted eternal life I'm afraid," said Alanna.

"Ken isn't all that hard to track down if you wanted to meet him,he's in Cousin' Jack's bar the high Street café most afternoons." "He's a legend said Lou in awe. "So is Cousin Jack," said Todd, "But that doesn't promise immortality." Jack is my first cousin said Lou quietly. "Well put it there," said Todd holding out his hand. Lou shook his calloused hand warmly. "We're originally from Silver City in Grant county New-Mexico," said Alanna, "We've been up here for twenty five years."

"I met a traveler from Eugene and he made up my mind to take U-Haul up here." Said Todd. "He thought there was another way to get involved with drug induced Hippies."

Jim told a joke, he said, "What do you get if you

cross a dwarf with a concrete mixer?" "I don't know what do you get plum pudding?" Said Louise. "A wee hardman," said Jim. Everyone started laughing at the Joke. Lou came back with a verbal riposte to her husband, "Did you hear about the wizard who went into a nunnery and said hocus pocus to one of the nuns. She replied forget the hocus just poke us." Everyone let out a natural involuntary laugh.

Todd and Alanna said they were going to get out and go home. "We'll speak again Lou and Jim," said Todd, "We'll see you in the High Street were the Nichols of Eugene," said Todd and Alanna. Jim noticed Todd was wearing a dark blue flecked lapis lazuli silver ring on his wedding finger it was really cool thought Jim.

They both said "Take care you two, no mad romping now." They took their naked bodies out of the hot spring and made their way towards the woods. Lou said, "What a cool couple Jim I would definitely like to see them again sometime." Jim replied, "The truth shocks you more than it does me reed; come let me bress yea in my arms." Lou went and sat in his arms,the bitch was content with a long loving embrace from her husband. She was cleansed and felt safe.

Carla was showered and had squeezed herself into her black Armani's it was a race against time to search out the fragile lightness of the day. She put on her crushed blue velvet brothel creepers and put on her white rose triumph brassiere. She brushed her teeth thoroughly for she had a gum infection Pyorrhea to be precise. She took Lady in her arms and cuddled her for she was her little child. The one she had never had. It was Carla that had infected Cousin Jack's testicles and then she also got hot ovaries. It was a very intimate delicate process that had taken place that night when they shared a bed. For Jack and Carla were, "Banes Common" way back far down the line. Suffice to say they had shared sexual congress on that night and it was forbidden love caught off the teeth. "Life is a ball alright," thought Carla in a tic.

The phone started ringing in that sad sickly weak traced American ring tone and Carla answered it. "Hey its Billy here." "I'll meet you in the red room in an hour," said Carla, "I'm getting dressed." Billy replied," Okay see you there in an hour partner." "I'm not prepared to forgive Cousin Jack for dobbing me in." Said Carla bitterly, "Okay toots we'll talk then," said Billy. "Bye now."
Just then a police siren sounded outside; Carla didn't know the double trouble she was setting herself up for. For Cousin Jack was part of the establishment—The Firm and she was just another trivial stranger.

Carla pulled on a clean black tee shirt and made up her face. She thought it's time to sup my tea and get out of here. She put Lady on her lead and left the dog to wonder around the apartment with its lead on. She thought "Hello hooray cousin Jack there's a price to pay for sending me to Jail." Of course like most criminals Carla was totally oblivious of her own guilt . . . the essential damage she had done to the kids.
Carla put on her faded blue Levi jacket picked up the dog and left the apartment.

Jim said to his wife, "Close your eyes long enough and the problem just disappears." "Well not this problem," said Lou angrily. "You are going to help me put that Carla back where she began, and that's a mental asylum." "Whatever you say darling," said Jim. "Did you know that her partner is an ex-mental health nurse and that she gets medication on the black market. She's a fucking space cadet that contains about as much originality as scraping dog shit off your shoe sole."

Carla walked up Powell past the Cherokee Motel.The Bates motel that never had any guests in the winter months. She then took a right onto Lexington and walked the four blocks up to the red room. The dog needed to do it's business and she stopped at the Lead bury exit. Lady suffered from constipation and Carla gave her "Dogalax" every morning. The little bitch did its hard little stool and Carla kicked the shit over the curb into the road channel.

Jim and Lou got out of the spring and toweled themselves dry. They then went and got dressed and walked quickly the four miles back to the car. It had been a perfect experience the hot springs. At the car Jim said to Lou, "Think of all the good times we are going to have. Baby I think it's alright driving through the timberline telling me you loves me." Lou replied, "Let's stop for a drink on the way home I know a log cabin on the way back where we can get a couple of cokes and sing an old country song."

They stopped at a bar called The Belmont. There were three or four Ford Helix's parked outside with guard dogs sleeping in the cabs. It was where the mountain men drank. They went in and four men were sitting at the bar drinking steam beer and sipping on Southern. Jim found the atmosphere slightly intimidating and they took two stools at the bar. A fat middle-aged woman was serving. She looked at them suspiciously because they weren't part of the Presbyterian caste. Jim pretty quickly realized she was as stupid as native Aberdonians- part of the same inbred group. Lou asked for two cokes and the barmaid went to get them. Jim was distracted by the intractable dialect of the Woman. It was Pepsi and she then opened the ring pulls with a massive hunting knife. Looking back it seemed so bizarre these people could only see so far. There was nothing to be afraid of although the men couldn't take their eyes off Lou.

Jim decides to break the tension and told a joke in his pure highland Scot's accent.

He said to Lou clearly and loudly, "Who's the fastest man on two legs in Biafra?" "I don't know replied Lou, "Who is he?" Jim smiled and said, "Carl Lewis chasing a bread van." Everyone laughed loudly and that was the tension over. Lou said, "We'll just let that fly stick to the wall". . .

Carla went into the Red Room and ordered a Miller. The bar was empty except for the barman. He knew her well and said "Hey how are yaw doing Carla?" "I'm good." She replied to him. She started coughing she would have to see the doctor about this cough-it wasn't looking good for her. She lit a red up and inhaled on the sustenance of the cigarette. She shivered from the base of her spine-it was cold and rimy today.

Billy arrived 5 minutes later. He was well over 6' tall and was a blue collar that had made it out of the housing project with his drug dealing. He had nothing to offer the world except drugs misuse and misery although he had a good sense of humor. In a tic he thrust his way to the bar,white urban working class trash on the make. The Pal TV was on, it was showing an edition of Peyton Place in keeping with the dark gothic surreal world that these two individuals inhabited. There was residual resentment on the barman's face because he didn't like Billy. He went over to Carla and ordered a shot of JD and a Miller lite. He lit up a camel Light and said to Carla, "You're looking nice today," and he went down and petted Lady because he wasn't without kindness to animals. Billy was a bit of a joker and he had heard a good joke in Casa U Bet You Bar last night. He said to Carla, "Do you want to hear a joke?" In his deep rough accent. He had brown eyes and one of his eyes had a milky caste on it.

Carla coughed her lungs up again and said between fits, "Yes, cheer me up Billy." He said "There was a guy on the Project who went into a bar to meet his best friend for a drink. He met the guy ordered a drink and said I've murdered my wife. The friend said I don't believe you and the guy said come up to my apartment and I'll show you. So they went up to apartment flat went through the close to the bum sitting out of the freshly dug earth. The friend said yeah you've murdered her right enough but why did you leave her bum unburied. The guy said, "I needed somewhere to park my bike". Carla burst into raucous laughter. The irony of Carla's bum was completely lost on both of them.

Carla said, "Let's go and get a seat where we can talk," and they took a seat way back in the winery darkness.

"I've got the gun," said Billy casually, "We'll black him out for good." "We take him out next month," said Carla smoking a cigarette. "He comes into The Blue Moon every last Friday before the end of the month to cash up, we kidnap him and take him to the hills and shoot him in the head." Said Carla with contempt. "We vaporize Cousin Jack on the 25th then," said Billy laughing nervously-for he had never killed a man before. "We get him outside at drinking up time when its real quiet, we'll be in mufti." "I've got the cuffs," said Billy, (for Billy wasn't beyond a little S&M with one of his little girlfriends) "We brutally crush that son of a bitch."

Calum Cumming

CHAPTER EIGHT

Lou and Jim left for their trip to Mexico on the 2nd of January 1992. Jim had checked the car the night before for water and oil and windscreen washer. They had packed the car and they left Swiss Cottage at first light 7AM. Pretty soon they were on the freeway and heading south. It was a foggy day and Jim had almost hit a runner in Eugene, because he was staring at her rear view and her wonderful ass. Eugene was the long distance running capital of America. Jim had thought about Madonna she was such a good runner. Lou had corrected him about soul sisters and then he had peered through the fog at the road ahead. Pretty soon they were making good time and they passed the ubiquitous Gas Food Lodgings sign every five miles or so. The freeway verges and surrounding fields were peppered with gaudy advertising. They passed a milk hoarding and Jim thought about Jayne Mansfield and her enormous mammary glands-1954 Miss New Jersey, she had died in a car accident.

They were still in the fog and they passed a London Fog Motel sign and nestled off the freeway was the motel on the right hand side. Jim suddenly felt a little homesick but Lou started singing and this cheered Jim up. They changed positions at fifty miles and Lou took over. A full tank would take them 250 miles all the way to Redding California where they were staying tonight. It was 600 miles and change to San francisco. They suddenly came to a turn off for a place for New Leeds and Jim said to Lou, "There was a young man from Leeds who swallowed a packet of seeds, great tufts of grass shot out of his arse and his balls were covered in weeds." Lou started laughing and said, "Cheeky." They were both listening to the radio and were content with the music. Lou had picked up some Oregon LSD mushroom from Grant on the 31st and she was planning on taking it in Mexico. She hadn't told Jim because he wouldn't have approved of that. He was so conservative she thought. He didn't like losing control. Pretty soon they came to some major roadworks and Jim saw that give way signs were illuminated and the horizontal arrows ascended lighting up right to left. There were intermittent red flares on the verge of the road instead of traffic cones for it was still misty.

Jim looked at the road being built there were no wooden profiles but steel pins with flags attached to each pin. This was the vertical and horizontal control of the road and each pin and its opposite was set out at 33 feet intervals. It certainly did give the smooth asphalt road a better slicker profile and Jim marveled at American civil engineering. It was cool and it seduced him.

They stopped for lunch at the Horn. They both had milkshakes and Spunkies hamburgers. Lou said to Jim over her strawberry milkshake, "It'll be dark when we get to Redding-we go over mount Shasta then down into Northern California at the Shasta Reservoir." "Suits me fine said Jim no tears goodbye this time." "We'll have our times apart Jim" said Lou, "But not for a very long time to come." Jim couldn't bear to be apart from his wife again for he had waited for her all his short life.

In a tic they were back on the freeway and heading for Mount Shasta. Suddenly a Shamen track "I Can Move Any Mountain came on the AM channel and Jim thought about his old friend Colin Angus from the Shamen,they had cracked America and he suddenly felt homesick again for Aberdeen. One Look at Lou lifted his mood though. He thought, "This is for the rest of our lives" Jim could feel unhappy sometimes but that was because of alcohol. Although Jim was calm he was also highly born and over sensitive. They went past some sheep in a field they were fat and woolly. Lou said to Jim nodding at the sheep, "Mary had a little lamb and it was always grunting,she tied it to a five bar gate and kicked it's little cunt in." Jim said, "Meh," loudly.

They went on down the freeway and Lou fell silent in repose, as she was wont to do. Jim said "A penny for your thoughts darling." Lou looked up and said, "I was thinking about Adam's sin and the fall of man." "He ate the flesh of the forbidden fruit and no longer were men and women naked in The Garden Of Eden." Said Jim. "Do you think that man exists in fall?" She said. "No Lou. I'm so very happy that you are mine-you are always on my mind." "But rain falls out of the sky-men fall in fighting!" Said Lou. "The rain pattern Lou is soul music Lou no-one really understands why that happens. It happened to me with you-it happened to Cousin Jack with Carla . . . all you can do is forgive and hope to forget about the fallout between people. It's not Armageddon time Lou and the four riders of the apocalypse" "I love you Jim." She kissed him on the cheek and Lou started crying softly the tears falling down her cheeks.

They drove on the rest of the afternoon and by four the car drove up Mount Shasta. They then drove down the other side into California. There was a famous diner at the roadside at the State border where people arriving in California would stop and eat and they stopped for a coffee and a sandwich. It was warm and Sunny,it would be dark in an hour and a half.

Lou said to Jim, "Welcome to California sweetheart." Jim replied laconically "California coming home." They then drove the car past Lake Shasta a huge artificial reservoir and dam. The scale was breathtaking. The water level was low, as it hadn't rained for over two years. It was the water supply for Northern California. The tidemark on the weetabix cliffs betrayed how low the water level was. Water in California was as precious as gold. The sum sparkled yellow in the late afternoon early evening.

Just before they made Redding at six o'clock Jim noticed a mass of molten metal at the side of the road and it glowed orange. That was a strange thing to see and it made him think about the movie star Warren Beatty. For orange is the color behooved of the womb. He couldn't explain why he thought about that and it left him perplexed.

It was the end of their day's journey and they were staying in the Blue Gum Motel. It was Jim's first experience of a Motel in America. The Motel was deserted and the swimming pool was empty under the neon sign in the darkness. They checked in giving their address in Eugene,they were in room nine.

They went into the room and Lou deadlocked the door behind her. She was a little tired after their first day traveling. There were two single beds a bathroom and a shower and a PAL TV. Lou turned on the bedside lights and pushed the beds together. She then shut the curtain. Jim turned on the blue screen light of the TV with the zapper. He found a Kevin Bacon movie he liked and left it on that channel. He lay on the bed and smoked a cigarette. Lou said to Jim "I've made a big decision today Jim I am going to have my coil removed when we get back to Oregon,what do you think?" "Do you want to have a baby Lou I mean we'll be parents then you know." Said Jim concerned. "It's a biological necessity Jim."

"We can use condoms until we're settled in and we have found a job," Said Jim, "Then we can try for a baby." "I suppose so," said Lou crestfallen. "I'm desperate for a baby honey it's once in a lifetime- give me a chance to break all the rules because I've got nothing to lose,give me a shot at the night,some kind of experience we can hold on to."

Jim decided to cheer Lou up and held her hostage in his arms. He said, "What's the difference between a policeman's truncheon and Paul Daniels wand?" "I don't know said Lou gunning, "Paul Daniels Wand is used for cunning stunts." Said Jim. Lou broke into a peal of laughter. Jim gave his wife a big poem. "Aunty Mary had a canary up the side of her drawers,it wouldn't come down for half a crown so she fed it a can of Coors. I made up the last line Lou."

"You really make me laugh Jim did you know that?" If you're not careful Lou I'll give you a fishy fanny as well." "Oh Jim," Said Lou supplying into his arms nice and tender like. She would always be sweet on her Jim she realized at once,it was an epigamic moment.

"I'll go and get us some beers and a cheeseburger and fries for supper Jim." "What kind of beers do you want Jim?" "Coors silver bullet brand Lou." "That sounded like a threat Jim!" She said. Lou stood up gathered up her bomber and the car keys and said, "I will be back."

Jim looked out the door it was pouring rain,it was a stormy foul night and he worried about his wife. It had rained in Lake Shasta for the first time in two years. Always take the weather with you,the cycle of replication like the brown irises of Cousin Jack's eyes,one disc partially obscured by the other fascinating.

Jim felt a little scared on his own he told himself a joke to cheer himself up. "Did you hear about the cross eyed teacher ... He couldn't control his pupils."

Jim lay on the bed and flicked the channels with the zapper. He found Marlon Brando and the Wild Bunch. The Drug store manager asks him what are you rebelling against and Brando replies "What have you got"? . . .

Jim suddenly heard a loud knock at the door.Lou had the keys and he wasn't about to answer the

door. The rain teemed down, the PAL TV droned on like a wasp. Jim Lay there rigid. He heard the person move off. He stood up and looked out the peephole into the blackness of the night. There was nobody there. He turned on the porch light for his wife and he felt reassured. He had just avoided a situation that would have gone pear shaped. Californian motels were the land of confusion.
There were too many men making too many problems and not enough love to go around.

Lou arrived back five minutes later with the beer and the burgers. The sound of her laughter and how he had held her tight seemed a long time ago. Jim told Lou about the knock at the door and she said," I bought a half jack of Jim Beam, as well it's sipping whisky." "Phew" said Jim. Lou's hair was wet and she dried it with the bath towel. It hung in shiny serpents. She laughed cruelly and said, "It's always good to hear the rain."

The next morning it was still raining and Jim and Lou showered and took their time over their ablutions. They went to hand in the motel keys and sign out. There was a policeman with a rain hat over his cap standing talking to the motel proprietor. There had been a murder the previous night. The night is full of holes and the Jim and Lou were at a place called vertigo. They decided to say nothing in Aberdonian fashion and quietly signed out.

They took off in the old Toyota and filled up with RON 90 Gas at the ubiquitous Mobil gas station. They got some coffee and chocolate dough rings for breakfast from Winchells.

They headed North on the freeway. Lou said they were making for Eureka on highway 101. It was on the coast and Jim would finally get to see the Pacific Ocean. They went past a field where two Bi planes were getting ready to take off on the rough grass. Lou said, "They are crop dusters that spray insecticide on the fields. They are Grumman Ag Cats piston prop engines." Jim replied "Charles Lindbergh eat your Amelia Ear hart out." Lou said she had thought of a joke that would make Jim laugh, she said, "Did you hear about the Irish terrorist? He thought muffin the mule was a form of sweaty cunnilingus." Jim replied Air Lingus.Paddy power!" Louise Lisa burst into laughter.

Pretty quickly they had headed off the freeway and were making for Highway 101,pacific highway. Eureka was a town of some 50,000 people and had made its money in the lumber industry and there had been gold discovered there in the Californian gold rush of the 19th century. Hence the name Eureka. It had made a lot of money in redwood. Like the port of Kinloch bervie in highland Scotland it made it's money in Lumber and fishing.

Some two hours later and they arrived in Eureka in Humboldt County. The pacific glistened light gray turquoise blue and Jim realized finally he had made it to the pacific rim of western civilization in a semi tropical climate-love in a mild climate. They checked into a motel on the edge of town. Jim saw an old guy in a pale blue Chrysler with all his belongings piled high up in the back. There was little or no social security for old people in the USA and this slice of Americana made Jim feel sad. The old birdman got out of the car with a poodle on its lead with red weary fur around her eyes. The dog was his soul mate and the man had to see what tomorrow would bring. He was staying in the motel tonight.

They checked into the cheap motel room $23 and decide to go down to the bay to see the ships. A red and white striped lighthouse was situated at the head of the port pier. Jim said to his wife Lou, "Port red, starboard green." There were small fishing boats and larger lumber boats that would take the lumber from the mill into their holds. The stripped piles of trees were scattered everywhere. It was Sunday and the massive overhead cranes were not working today. It was the stevedore's day off. Lou held Jim's hand and was interested in the boats, she had a real gutsy lust for life Louise. Jim said to his wife, "When my father and mother were on honeymoon in Belfast my father had said to my mum I love boats but you would not understand that." "What a cruel thing to say to your new wife Jim as if really he didn't want to understand his wife!" Said Lou. Jim replied "A blasted at the root unusual ballsy cynic who could have achieved anything if it wasn't for that damned whisky bottle." "Well we're here now let's go and get a beer in one of the harbor bars." Said Lou.

They walked back and went into Dinos. There was pop music playing and it was exclusively male. Jim ordered two Miller Lites and they took their seats at the bar. Just as they got their order a female voice spoke from a small stage recessed beside the door. The voice said, "Hi I'm Lindsey." They both looked round to their left and saw a naked young middle aged woman with a diamante banded cowboy hat on pole dancing. Her vagina was shaved and she was turning on the old lounge lizards for dollars playing with her wrinkly vulva. She said, "I love your accent Scotchman can I dance for you." Lou said, "Welcome to California honey looking directly into Jim's eyes. He just grinned and stared at the pole dancer for what seemed an eternity. Lou was more than a match for the advancing nubile and said "Back off buster papoose tits or I'll kick you in the fud you little tart." Jim started laughing and the old guys cheered. They soon found themselves outside on a Eureka street. Jim said, "These things aren't exactly startling to an Aberdonian velvet crabber Lou." She replied, "These are supposed to be the things we lost in the fire of our marriage Jim." Jim replied droopily, "I suppose so wifely."

Carla hadn't stopped crying-her uncle had died the night before in Tacoma bay, Seattle, Washington state. She had been so close to her uncle her mother's brother. In a tic she realized that she and her brother Al would inherit a lot of money for her paternal uncle Ray Charles had been a watchmaker he had been one quarter black American and had been a hard diligent pawnbroker. She realized as she rolled a joint with her little arty fingers that Bill with income was coming over that afternoon and she finally realized that she wanted to bury her drug dealing for she would inherit some $100,000 and she would be a rich women. But she still had a beef with Cousin Jack,she had suffered in prison as a result of her own criminality. Something she was blinkered to when it came to Cousin Jack. But Jack was having an Indian summer. . .

Jim and Lou went up to Safeway's near the motel to buy some food and beer. Outside was a brightly painted Totem pole. The carved phallic symbol rose high up towards the blue sky. They came across a Native American collecting soda cans in a cart beside the shopping mall's entrance. He must have been about 50 and had beautiful hair. It was lustrous and black chestnut straight down his back. The rear view. "Hey Dude," said Lou and the man turned around and eyed them with some suspicion for there wasn't much room for the beaten down tribes off the reservation. There was no place for them there outside Safeway's. Lou said "Are you selling those soda cans for dollars," and she pointed at the shopping cart. "I redeem them for money if I work hard enough I can make enough to eat that day." He then stayed quiet and stood up straight. Jim noticed he had strong features,a strong nose and chin. Lou said, "Which tribe are you?" He replied magnificently with black brown eyes, "Iroquois I don't drink or smoke grass young lady. I came off the reservation about six months ago looking for work." Jim could see how proud he was and his obvious surprise to find two young whites that would take an interest in him. "My name is Running Wolf nice to meet you." Jim shook his hand and said "Jim and Lou Running Wolf." Jim offered him a cigarette and surprisingly he accepted it for there was always something he liked about Scotsmen. Jim sparked him up and Running Wolf took a deep grateful lungful. "Here keep the pack said Jim to the Indian. "No I couldn't do that," Demurred Running Wolf. "No I insist," said Jim. "Are you going to go back to the reservation Running Wolf," said Lou "No I don't think," so said Running Wolf. Lou could tell that he was running away from something but she wasn't going to wound his pride by questioning him further. "Let us buy you some food Running Wolf." Said Lou. He said "No I don't beg," "It's not begging," said Lou "Just an act of gratitude to you and native America." "I'll just have a sandwich then," he said looking downwards.

Jim and Lou went into the store and bought some beer and food they came out about 5 minutes later with his sandwich but he had disappeared. "OH Jim" said Lou; "We offended him with our honky hospitality." "He'll be alright said Jim optimistically.

They went up to the motel room to eat their sandwich. Lou was strong and silent for she felt intensely sorry for Running Wolf but there was nothing she could do,he had made his choice and she realized that his strength of character had buoyed her,he was mentally tough and a free spirit. In the land of the free and the home of the brave.

Running Wolf had redeemed his cans and had got $5 enough for a cheap meal. He went down to the Fisherman's mission at the quayside for his soup and a sandwich. The Iroquois were one of the five nations of America and there was the most important role of the mother in their philosophy. They believed in the league of peace and freedom, which underpinned their values. Running Wolf wondered as he ate his soup why does white man always have to be right.

Jim and Lou ate their sandwich and watched PALTV it was BILLY starring Billy Connolly,he also believed in peace and freedom and felt condemned by the fact that there was such a peripheral role for the mother in Scottish society. All the male Scottish writers just seemed interested in the wee holy wily book of Calvinism. Billy had cracked America and had left the native pain of Scotland behind, for now. But as any famous person knew it was difficult to avoid the pain sometimes. You had to be impregnable like a panzer tank.

Billy arrived in the midafternoon. He had driven over. He was the same age as Carla and he looked his years with his tonsure. Carla and Billy addressed one another. "I've got last week's take with me, it's $10,000 in fifties. You owe me $1,000 for last week Carla." Carla felt devastated for she thought she had done nothing wrong. Even though she was responsible for having sent many people into hospital with drug induced psychiatric problems. She had done her time and she wanted out. "Because I admitted the offence I got a reduced sentence for dealing MDMA cut with hexamine . . . I want out Billy I got in with the wrong crowd It's common for people working in bars to become drug mules of class A drugs, that is how I found you Billy working in a bar." She looked at him and suddenly realized how much she hated him. "Right" she said "No more dealing Billy."

"Drugs has a wider appeal for me than that Carla it's a chance to enjoy the good life." His patter was really good she thought He was bound for inglorious defeat. "Most people who take MDMA have fallen in with the wrong crowd Billy I don't want to prey on young people any longer." Said Carla. "I'll pay you off for this week and that's it. I've inherited an inheritance from my uncle in Tacoma bay, I don't need the money anymore. I'll give you the business."

Billy looked at her with his caste brown eyes they were like a China mans eyes, slanted and slits. "You won't have any credibility anymore Carla," said Billy. Let's go to O' Neal's Irish bar and we can talk without drawing any heat from the law. "I don't have any idea of what's going on in your head just now Carla."

Carla agreed to go to O' Neal's with Billy. She took the money and her business checkbook with her,she had a fictitious beauty Modeling business and she would pay the money into the account on the way over to O'Neal's. She paid Billy off. He had hard fists and a small brain. She thought to herself after today I go straight. She thought she should do it. The money was paid into Carla's modeling account on the way over. It was dirty money. Billy said to Carla in the car "What do we do about cousin Jack Carla?" "We'll talk about that in O'Neal's" said Carla. They went into the up market bar diner and got an order of beer. It was not what girls were supposed to do order beer in pubs during the day. Billy said," I'll tell you an Irish joke Carla." "Keep your voice down Billy this bar is full of Irish." Billy laughed and said certainly madam. "There was an Irishman working on a skyscraper in New York and he opened his sandwiches, he had cheese and onion chips, the next day he opened his sandwiches and he had cheese and onion chips. The third day he opened his sandwiches and he had cheese and onion chips- Then he threw himself off the top of the Hi Rise and was found dead. At the funeral his wife said he should have made his own sandwiches!" Billy guffawed loudly at his own joke.

This bar had European Sky television it was on soccer and the English premier league, it was a charity match between Manchester United and

Blackburn Rovers. Carla looked at the goggle box it was a Green Shield stamps cum dividend charity select game and she could have sworn that one of the players in Man U colors was the singer Morrissey from the Smiths,he had distinctive sideburns and he was young and athletic. He grinned at them and winked. Watching me watching you. It was all part of the master plan leading to world harmony . . . MOZ.

Carla said to Billy "I don't want the word put out on cousin Jack but you take him on the 25th I'll kick his teeth out and he won't have that 24 carat smile any longer." "What do I do with the heater Carla I got it legally." "Sell it Billy we wont get away with murder." "You've fairly changed your tune Carla what brought this on?" "I want to do some good with what's left of my life I have this terrible cough". . . "Pack in the smokes Carla."

Jim and Lou took off early the next morning they were making for Santa Rosa some 200miles drive. At the route 101 run in they saw Running Wolf trying to hitch a lift. Jim was driving and he stopped to pick him up. "How's it going Running Wolf where are you going." He replied "Southern California." Jim said we could take you as far as Santa Rosa. "Okay" he said, "I come with you." He had a roll knap and a rucksack on his back. Running wolf got in the car and sat erectly in the back seat. "Hi Lou" he said. "I'm sorry about yesterday Lou but I don't beg." "That's alright," said Lou, "I understand. Where did you sleep last night, rough?" "I slept in the fisherman's mission at the quayside."

"We have some bread cheese and polish sausage

we can share our breakfast with you." "Okay" said Running Wolf "I would like that." Lou made him a sandwich and realized she had broken the ice. They made good time and soon they had arrived at a town called Willis to get gas for the car. Jim pumped gas and two Hells Angels pulled in on their motorcycles. Their knapsacks were tied to the rear of the seat of the chrome Harley Davidson stallions. They filled up with gas. Jim watched them-it was a myth. A piece of urban west coast Americana. Jim checked out their colors they were MC members Long Beach they were from Los Angeles. They wore polka dot welder's bandanas on their heads and had on mirror shades. They paid for their gas and took off with a loud burble. Easy laid back in the saddle with their whiskers in the wind. They headed North on Route 101. Jim paid for the gas and came back with three coffees. Running Wolf was telling Lou a joke and Jim was in time to hear it. Lou said, "What have you got Running Wolf?" "Did you hear about the man who was drinking in a bar in Long Beach Los Angeles? After 20 aftershocks he couldn't find his house." "There's a big one coming that god dam San Andreas Fault line."

They shared a couple of smokes and drank their coffee. Jim said to Running Wolf, "Where are you headed Running Wolf," He said, "Frisco." Jim said "Where all the people wear flowers in their hair." "What will you do in San Francisco Running Wolf?" I've fallen through the net there is no way back in the USA once the safety trampoline has been removed, I is no trapeze artist. It's either collect cans in the sunshine or get the blues back on the Indian reservation." "Why don't you let me help you Running Wolf I can see that you're a proud honest man,but pride comes before a fall." Said Lou. "I can get you work up in Eugene with my cousin Jack Macleod." She said. "Are you related to cousin Jack," said Running Wolf." "He is a good man my uncle. He is the richest hippy in Oregon He has spirit,he's a legend." "He's my uncle," repeated Lou, "Why don't you let us buy you a greyhound ticket in Santa Rosa? I'll call him he'll get you work and somewhere to stay." "Call it a present to Native America from Scotland" said Jim, "You're not so different from the Scots,materially poor but honest and rich in soul."

"Did you know," said Running Wolf that Amazing Grace is a Native American song?" "Grace is courage under pressure,Running Wolf, please let us help you." Said Lou. "Wail is Native American music," Said Running wolf. "Chicken scratch is the foundation of Dixieland blues and hip hop music." "The native American suffers from more alienation and racial abuse than black man." Said Running Wolf. "I know that," said Lou, "But cousin Jack understands that he'll be patient with your life."

"How did you get the name Running Wolf?" Said Jim. Running Wolf said, "When I was a young boy I was lazy my father had to drive me out of bed every morning by rapping my shins. One morning he scolded me hard and said I should be out hunting Deer. When my father left the teepee I asked the tribal seer to make a buckskin mask for me. He made me a mask and I spent the day painting it with white clay and fixing deer horns to it. Before sunrise the next morning I was the first out of bed and took my father's gun and knife and rode away on a horse with two led horses behind me. I went out to a little lake near the village and fastened the horses. In the wood and then went down to a place where animals came to drink. When the sun rose some deer came there but they did not run away because they thought I was a deer. I killed two and loaded them on the horses. And brought them home just as my father was waking up.

My father told me I had done well and we divided the venison with our neighboring tribe. The next morning I went back to the watering place and returned with two more deer. And the morning after that I did the same. My father told me to stop or I would smell like a deer.

I began sleeping late again and my father scolded me rapping me on the shins. My father told me I could no longer use the family horse if I wanted a ride. He told me I would have to take one from the other tribe. That morning as my father went hunting I went to the seer and asked her if she would make me a new pair of moccasins. She did this for me and spent the day decorating them with beads and paint in a special way. At sundown I left the teepee with my gun and returned with twenty wild unbroken horses. Over the next four days I returned with over 120 wild unbroken horses. My father was much pleased and after my father died I got a new teepee made for me and I painted my teepee black. I tied feathers to the door and other finery around to signify that I was a great warrior.

"Come in to my teepee," I said to her in Crow. The moonlight was full and Red Shield felt her heart beat strongly, I saw her then and said in Crow "Come in" but she did not understand Crow and she neither answered me nor moved. I shrugged and went inside. Red shield heard me say something else and the voice of an old woman responded.

Red shield arose then and went into the teepee. The fire had died to a few coals and Red shield could only make out my shadowy form and my mother. She went close to the fire as if to warm her. The old woman spoke to Red shield and told her to take off her moccasins and rest in crow. But red shield did not understand. I built up the fire so I could see her face. She was the woman of my dreams,I had dreamt about her often. She was a brave Sioux warrior and she had come to me to offer herself up as my wife. We had united the Sioux and the Iroquois maternal tribes she was my wife and after that our two tribes lived in peace on the reservation."

"So where is Red Shield then?" Said Lou concerned. "She is in Oregon State mental hospital. She has Schizoid Affective disorder. A chance encounter with fate fed with whisky, marijuana and cocaine. "Oh running wolf," said Lou "I'm so sorry you must let us help you so you can be near your wife,white man has fed you and your family enough snake oil- fucking carpet braggers." "I'll take you up on your offer then if cousin Jack can get me a job." "Do you know I think you will be very popular with Jack Running Wolf? I'll call him when we get to Santa Rosa." Said Lou.
They made Santa Rosa about 4.30 PM and went straight to the greyhound bus station down town. Santa Rosa was all stucco white like most of the old timer Spanish influenced Southern Ca. Lou put a call through to Cousin Jack in Eugene. At the High Street café. He answered the phone personally.

"Hi Jack its Lou here is everything fine?"
"Hell yes, Little Lou."
"I have a proposition for you Cousin Jack."
"Fire away Lou I'm all ears."
"We ran into an Iroquois American in Eureka and now were in Santa Rosa."
"Yeah Lou". . .
"Red Shield his wife is in Salem State Mental Hospital with Bi-polar; can you help him get his wife out of hospital and give him a job,his name is Running Wolf?"
"I'm looking for a driver,Lou,does Running Wolf have a driver's license?"
"I'll let you speak to him Cousin Jack-hold the line."
"Mmm Yeah Lou". . .
"Hi Cousin Jack Its Running Wolf speaking."
"Are you coming up to Eugene,Running Wolf,on the greyhound bus, I mean."
"That was the plan,Jack,the bus gets in tomorrow at nine AM."
"I have a Driver's License or I can Labor for you I'm looking for a way to get my wife out of Salem State Mental Hospital so we can go back onto the Reservation."
"You can drive for me Running Wolf and stay with my Movie house partner,Clay,and his wife Vicky until things are settled with your wife Red Shield. Would that suit you,any friend of Lou's and Jim's is a friend of mine". . .
"That would be perfect Cousin Jack,if there is anything I can do for you just name it."
"It's always good to have a new face on the board, Running Wolf". . .
"I'll meet you at the greyhound bus station in Eugene tomorrow at nine."
"You bet yaw,Jack,thank you."

JACK NICHOLSON

"Don't thank me I know the way crap is poured on top the native Americans, you must be a clan chief with a name like that."
"Yes . . . that's right . . . a clan chief Jack."
"Alright till tomorrow then bye."
"Goodbye Cousin Jack and good wishes to you."
Lou took the phone and said to Jack-"Thanks Cousin- I really appreciate you helping out Running Wolf,there is a safety net after all." "Friends help out honest friends that's all Lou-you and Jim take care in LA and Baja"
"Yeah, bye Jack." "Bye Lou." And Lou put down the phone. "Lou that is so kind of you I won't forget your kindness you know." Said Running Wolf. "Its all part of the new deal," said Jim "A kick against the pricks as Johnny Cash put it bluntly"
Lou took Running wolf's rucksack and said "C'mon lets get you on the bus." She said Cousin Jack is 76 now but he has the mind of a young man and loves young people you'll get on great with him." Jim said laconically "Did you hear about the Flasher that flashed at three pensioners? The first two pensioners had a stroke and the third one couldn't reach." Running Wolf smiled - Shyly for cheap titillation was not part of his repertoire. They left him standing in line for the bus and Lou gave him $5 for a sandwich. She wouldn't take a refusal from Running Wolf. He shook hands with them so politely and Lou said "See yaw in Eugene, Running Wolf." "Yes until then," replied Running Wolf.
They took off in the old silver Toyota Corolla.They was staying with Sean and Jill McLeod tonight. Sean was a trainee fireman with the San Francisco Fire Dept. and Jill worked for a construction coy. Jill's father was a Canadian,a Mackenzie. Jill had been Lou's best friend at Ventura High School.

Lou had told Jim that as a young girl Jill had suffered from Scoliosis and had titanium rod in her spine-she was a hero. Lou told Jim she was beautiful and was a very sassy young lady who could have made it in Hollywood.

They arrived just as it was getting dark and it was warm and balmy. Lou introduced Jim to Sean and Jill,she really was beautiful and looked a little like a cross between Edie Sedgwick and Jessica Lange.

Jill and Sean welcomed them in,it was beginning to get dark and the air was warm and dry as tinder. Jill brought through some Rolling Rock beers, they were tired after their drive. The beer was invigorating. Jill said to Jim "I hear you are a civil engineer Mr. Cumming-you could get some work with my Brothers if you decided to come to Southern Ca. they have their own civil engineering contractor in Ventura." Jim replied, "I think were bound for Portland up in Oregon but the offer if it is still there may be a bonus in the future." Sean was smoking and said that car suits you guys, pasta and pizza." "Yeah it's great," said Lou. Sean said there had been a murder in the neighborhood last night. He said, "It's when it happens around you that you start getting worried, the neighborhood watch isn't much reassurance." Jim looked around the living room in the Californian stucco bungalow,it was a pared down living style pastel minimalism. It looked a story of reinvention for this glamorous young couple. Jim had been ratty with Lou before they arrived the driving had taken its toll on him and he badly wanted to apologize to his beautiful and stunning wife. Jim went to the bathroom and took a long piss. He inadvertently left the door open and he heard Jill shout through, "I like a man with a good riddle Jim." He smiled, he really liked this young fresh couple. Lou went to use the bathroom and freshen up. Jim apologized to her for their spat. Lou said, "You can be very bad tempered sometimes,Jim,the young destroyer." "I try to control my rise,it's just sometimes the pressure deforms my head like a vice around my skull I don't' mean to take it out on you." Said Jim. "Apology accepted Jim but we have to have a situation of downright equality where you always place my love for you first." She kissed him on the nose and pinched his sexy bottom.

Jim went back through to his beer and told them about Running Wolf and cousin Jack. Jill said "It's cousin Jack that found this house for us,he sourced it for the two of us. Lou came back from the bathroom and sat down to her beer. There was static in the air and Lou got a shock on her bum. Sean said, "Its static electricity,sparks will fly Lou." "Did you get a sore bum sweetheart?" said Jim. Lou said to Jill, "When are you planning to start a family Jill?" Jill replied assuredly "We will start a family when Sean is trained as a fireman. We want to have a lot of kids." "I just want two," said Lou with equal certainty. Jim was left a little dismayed for he wanted honey blossom all to himself. Children were for grown-ups. Jim said, "It's unusual that both you and Lou are McLeod's Sean? Are you from Scotland originally?" said Jim. "My family came from the Isle of Skye originally." Said Sean, "I've worked there," said Jim, "It's a magical place and the blood is strong the heart is highland." Lou's family was from Leodhas in Na hearadh. It seems the Leo lion plays a large part in Scottish life,Jim said Jill. For she was a Skye Mackenzie. From Manitoba originally in the met agama from the old world. Jim's Mackenzie roots were from point in Lewis. "The Lion Rampant," said Jim, "The color of sienna and crop added Jim. "The idealistic color of LA" said Lou we're all part of you, darling. "Donald's yellow ice cream in Aberdeen," said Jim to his wife. They were all agreed that chiefly Leo McLeod was a most unusual and decent sensitive clan of people.

The conversation had placed Lou's star firmly at the top of the Christmas tree.

Jill and Lou went through to the kitchen in the bungalow to fix up the enchilada dinner with salad. Sean said to Jim," I heard you were a cyclist Jim." "Before my brief motorcycling days I loved cycling. said Jim. I have a racing bike said Sean, do you want to see it? It's out in the garage." "Sure," said Jim, "I'd love to." They went out to the garage it was a colnago painted in metallic yellow and blue. The bike was campanology throughout; And Jim could smell the rubber of the tubs and glue holding them to the rim. The chain was gold plated and well oiled.

Sean's Helix was sitting in the garage it was silver- Jim and Lou's favorite color, the color of candy. They went in and had dinner with some Napa red wonderful smells of Victoria plum and autumn fruits.

Running Wolf relaxed into his 14hour journey he was sitting next to a black Woman who was going from LA to Seattle in Washington State. She showed him her hunting knife and Running Wolf said it needed sharpening a little as it was they shared a meal of Matteson's smoked sausage, cheese and rye. Hales the old black squaw gave him a drink of her cool potable water from her melted ice fruit jar. They shared a Salem menthol cigarette. In an instant Running Wolf promptly fell asleep where he would not wake until they had reached Salem at 7AM and he was within touching distance of his wife Red Shield. It was instinctive-he was less than two miles from his wife and a glow arose in her heart as she dreamt in the early morning sunshine of her husband. The clan chief Running Wolf.

She had been given an injection of Clod pixel Ace phase the liquid cash over a week ago and she no longer ran with the mad rabble or chopped up her jeans with scissors. The young Squaw Sioux had retreated into the folklore of a quiet place where she wanted to be with her own people on the reservation. Her condition had been stabilized and Jack thought about her the brown disc of one eye partially obscured by the caste of another soul.

Carla woke early and fed Lady some cold sausage with biscuits for she needed roughage. If Carla had realized then Christ would save her from a death from cancer-radiotherapy would save her although there were no guarantees in life-accept able Carla.

She had met a wonderful man in the Red Room last night-his name was Mannie Kennedy and the deformation of his character had suggested to her that in some sense he was nursing a broken heart-his fairytale had not come true. He was a strong man with Sea blue eyes and curly long golden blonde hair. He had told her that he was a barrel maker with the Macmenamin brewing coy. He was easy meat so she thought.

Carla had gone to bed with him for she also was a troubled soul and was in need of succor. Mannie had suckled her wonderful breasts and had filled her up with his large elegant schilling.

And now they were left with the recriminations of the morning. Although it wasn't going to be that way for Mannie had fallen in love with Carla. He rose and scratched the hair on his chest. Carla said to him, "Would you like me to suck you off Mannie?" He said to her in a tic". . . No darling you were wonderful last night." "Alright, my lung hurts I have an appointment at the hospital tomorrow which I have to keep." Mannie drew the curtains a fine mist of wet beads of bullet water was on the window as they stared into the gray day.

Jim took a ride with Sean in his pickup the next morning. They rode over the speed bumps and Jim had clung on when they rode them with a bump. Jim said to Sean, "In Britain speed bumps are known as sleeping policemen," and Sean thought it was the funniest thing in the world. The down town west was high tech and modern and Sean told Jim his partner Walt Sax was a professional baseball player with the local side. Originally he was from East Coast Michigan and he was the real thing.

Sean had a printing job to do in Prontaprint and he told Jim that Jill had once photographed her breasts in a printer in Colorado when she had had to go there with her job once for a week. "It kept me going Jim." He said to Sean what's your star sign Sean?" "Virgo/Ape," said Sean nonchalantly. "Friday the 13th 1968." He added. "That means virility and long life," said Jim "I'm Taurus/Tiger. Friday the 18th 1962." Sean concentrated on the photo printer and said as he worked, "So that means virility and long life if you don't get squashed by a cop crossing the speed bumps horned man". . .

Running Wolf made it into Eugene Bus Station right on schedule at 9AM. Cousin Jack was waiting for him and Running Wolf shook his hand and excused himself,he had to loosen his bowels in the bathroom. He watched the faeces flush away in the Mannie and wondered what sort of crap his wife Red Shield was in.

It was a mild sunny day and running Wolf wished that he were out hunting with the dogs on the Reservation. The Estate for the Reservation was the Indian icon of Project Shell Housing in places like North East Chicago or Pittsburgh.

He washed his hands and face with warm water, soap, lathered and felt better. He took out his new orange and white clipped safety razor and shaved the soft auburn hair on his redskin face. Cousin Jack came into the bathroom and said "Oyo You can have a shower at the High Street café later today. Let's go for breakfast first, we'll go to the egg and spoon on Broadway. We can talk about your wife and what we can do to free her."

"I've arranged to meet an old partner of mine, The merry prankster Ken Kesey in the high Street café this afternoon,he has good connections in Oregon State Mental Hospital,he is dating Kathryn Morse a senior psychiatrist there." Jack was 5' 11" and was dwarfed by the size of Running Wolf. He looked up to Running Wolf shaving. "Is she redwood Cousin Jack I mean can I trust them."

"Hell yeah, Running Wolf, she's half Ken's age and that old oculist is on his second liver. Kathryn believes in a holistic approach to mental health. It's got to be proactive Running Wolf." He had finished shaving and recognized Native American in brown-eyed Jack,it was an innocent intuitive recognition in both men. For Jack's hair had once been Cherokee chestnut. As Jim might have commented about his roots in Aberdeen where he possessed just shades of Beaker blood.

Mannie Kennedy got dressed and gently let Lady the pet Chihuahua nip his finger tips,she was a charming little creature and the dog and it's short life suddenly forced Carla and Mannie to consider awhile their own sense of mortality. "How old is she?" said Mannie. "She's six," said Carla-"middle aged like her mistress." "I'm 51," said Mannie. "I'm 30ish," lied Carla and she let out a giggle. Mannie looked at her and chose to say nothing. She calmed down and said solemnly, "It's team past it this time I'm too old to breed now." "But you have your life Carla; surely that isn't over in the tic of a kettle."

"I cough up blood Mannie . . . in the morning." "You are not going to die Carla I can tell that,you have strong genes. You didn't get that black curves figure for nothing. Good African genes Carla." "That's completely right," reflected Carla and she suddenly felt better about herself.

"Let me get dressed, Mannie, and I'll make you some bacon and eggs and we can talk. Would you like

more coffee"? . . .
"Yeah that would be fine, my love." Said Mannie, and he looked fondly at her with his sea-blue eyes.

When Jim and Sean got back from Prontaprint Lou and Jill were gassing over coffee. They were watching Frazier on TV and Kelsey Grammar was stuck with Granddad in the New York apartment. Jim watched the TV for a second or two and realized suddenly he had never met cousin Jack's children, Jennifer and his daughter by his second marriage, Rebecca. They both lived in LA. Jennifer was a wardrobe artist and Rebecca had married into the Coleman's English mustard empire. They both had kids and Jack had wished that he could spend more time with his grandchildren. For Jack had realized long ago that that was all there was and he had realized so much in a shining moment of epiphany. The road of the unconverted on the road to Damascus when Saul turned to Paul.

Lou said, "We're having cheeseburgers for lunch does that suit you treacle features?" "Thank you, Jill that would be great," said Jim politely. He sat down opposite Sean and said to him, "What is it like to be in the fire brigade, Sean?" He recited the manual and said, "Firefighting is primarily to extinguish hazardous fires that threaten property and civilian or natural populations and to rescue people from dangerous situations like collapsed or burning buildings." "You must have to practice a lot," said Jim. "We practice all the time," said Sean. "Do you have a rope?" Said Lou. "All firefighters carry a standard 30 foot rope, Lou, so you can escape from burning buildings." Said Sean. "25% of all fatalities to fire fighters are caused by vehicles responding to an incident. Kind of ironic no?" Added Sean.

Cousin Jack and Running Wolf were in the High Street café at 2PM. Running Wolf had a 7 UP and Jack contented himself with an iced coke. Running Wolf had had a shower and change of clothes. The old warrior felt better for he was a cleanly man next to godliness.

Ken and Kathryn sauntered into the bar and came up to Cousin Jack. Ken said, "The closest I get to the Native American is now." He introduced himself to Running Wolf and shook his hand warmly laying his hands on his shoulders. Kathryn said "Hi" shyly from behind. Cousin Jack the handpicked Joker said "Hi Hi" to them both. Kathryn started laughing consistently and she ordered a couple of bottles of Diamond White cider from the barman.

Running Wolf was interested in Ken for he had read "One Flew Over The Cuckoos Nest" when his wife had been sectioned into the mental health asylum system. He said to him, "Your book is the most fantastic story of the oddest people collected together." "It's ultimately a love story of honor, Running Wolf." Said Ken. "I'm already working on Red Shield's case," said Kathryn who had returned from the bar with the cider. "Her story resonates with me and there is going to be a happy ending from her misery."

Jack told a joke and lifted the situation-"What's the difference between MADONNA and the gamble of a horse drawn coffin carriage? "I don't know what is the difference?" Said Kathryn. "The difference is," said Jack, "Is that Madonna has more clout than a horse's one unlucky gold plated shoe."

"My problem is cooking Kathryn, I can't cook for myself," said Running Wolf in reply.

"Lots of people can't cook Running Wolf but I can see you are a calm person." Said Kathryn. "The groups of patients in Salem State hospital have turned against Red Shield because she is a redskin," said Ken "They will do anything to catch the doctor's attention and gain respect." Added Kathryn. She pulled out a file and put on her glasses and opened it.

She said, "It's this," and she pondered for a second or two. "When I started reading Red Shield's case I was completely moved." She stifled a few tears and continued, "Her loss is more important to me than any other patient I have ever come across for Red Shield is a Sioux chief's daughter." "I can tell you now that her father feels broken and has nothing more to live for without his daughter." Said Kathryn. "There's no justice in this world," said Ken taking a swig on his cider.

Jim and Lou went and had a sleep after lunch for they were storing up sleep and both of them always needed a lot of sleep. They took all their clothes off and went to bed. Lou cuddled lovingly into Jim and they slept relaxed in the safety of Sean and Jill's home for three hours. When they woke up Jim tenderly bent down and kissed his wife's vulva before they got dressed. The feint lingering odor of his wife's slit smelt wonderful. Lou said, "You can make love to me tonight Jim.I'll massage your back,Jill has some healing aromatherapy almond oil that I can use." Jim looked forward to that for his wife had strong good hands and already he felt aroused what with all the cumin inside of him.

Cousin Jack and Ken had got into a friendly argument about Kurt Vonnegut and "Slaughterhouse Five." The novel was based loosely around Vonnegut's experience as a POW in Dresden after he had been captured at the Battle of the Bulge in WW2. Vonnegut had been imprisoned in a slaughterhouse and this acted as a metaphor for the destruction of war. It is a ringing testimony to the utter uselessness of war and Vonnegut. WW2. Vonnegut and his fellow POWs' was liberated by the brutal revenge of the Russians and they in turn became the enemy of the USA in the cold war.

Vonnegut is a third generation German and understands German culture and language. He is a humanist pacifist.

Jack said, "Look at Neal Cassady he used the male hammer knocking in the iron pins on the railroad as a metaphor for standing up for your rights, Ken." "Yeah but he was a real handful a slab of rotten meat at the end." Said Ken dismally. Running Wolf had been listening to them and was encouraged to join in and say something. "He said you have to fight for your wife's rights to no longer be used by white party people invading the reservation."

Kathryn said "My grandfather was the inspiration for the factory foreman in Schenectady in Slaughterhouse Five," That is how Ken and I got talking in here one night, and we fell in love." "Whole entities as opposed to the sum of their parts," said

JACK NICHOLSON

Jack. "That is why slaughterhouse five is a failed novel of sum parts." Said Kathryn.

"Where it doesn't matter what kind of healing chemicals are found running through your blood stream. Holism," said Running Wolf. "Holy stone, a soft sandstone that is used in rubbing the timber decks of ships," said Ken. "Or to consider the Papacy the Holy See which is the court of the Roman Catholic church." Said Ken, for he had been interested once in organized world religion. He looked up at Running Wolf,his two different names and he realized how much he admired and loved the history of the North American Indian.

"I know you Mannie replied, "Yes certainly-you're going to have to stop smoking Carla-pot as well." Carla had taken his strong arm and suddenly thought about her first boyfriend Dermot O' Leary and his strength of character; for Mannie was not unlike him.

"My appointment is at the Belmont Hospital tomorrow at eleven AM-will you come with me Mannie?" He picked up the signals and replied "Of course my love."

They went with Lady and disappeared into the blackness of The Red Room where they had met last night. They had some lunch and Carla bought a bottle of champagne. They felt like the German brave young crew of Das Bootee before they set out on their first mission from La Rochelle.

Jim, Lou, Sean and Jill went to an Italian restaurant. Canales for supper that night out on the coast. The food was good although the place was stressful. Over dinner Lou said to Jill, "I don't feel safe in here, all these people coming and going, is it a front for the Cosa Nostra?" Sean butted in and said, "You bet little Lou." Meanwhile Jim was tucking into his clam vogue and spaghetti. Jill said, "Mafia families and blood families like the LA Cripps are distinct enemies. The old boy Louie Canale who owns this joint owns a Casino in Atlantic City. Before he came out to the coast, his front over there was a café on the Boardwalk, the Washington Café. The casino was the home of Northern Soul dancing on the East Coast of America." Sean said," Like the LA Cripps Louie Canale has managed to escape prosecution more often than would be expected." Sean pointed and said "That's him over there." Lou looked over her shoulder and saw an old bald Italian boy in a cloud of cigarette smoke talking to a young man who was polishing a saxophone.

"The young guy is his son Budgie, his anointed successor who works here on slave wages." "He has an older son Michael but he lost honor and won't be getting his hands on the empire." Why?" Said Lou. "He tried to gas himself and his baby children with car fumes in a Pontiac Firebird one time and currently he is in San Quentin prison. "What would a father want to do that for?" Said Jim astounded. Louie had him working as a croupier in the Casino in Atlantic City and his wife and kids were here out on the coast. She used to do tricks with guys for some spending money." Said Sean and he let out a giggle. "You can imagine the rest Lou," Said Jill with a happy looks on her beautiful coupon.

"He has a daughter Suzie she is a real wild ridge as

well, she's a heroin addict and lives with her squalid little boyfriend in San Francisco." Said Jill who had almost finished her tortellini. "Her boyfriend Raymond Little is one of the weakest people I have ever met in my life. Pure junkie scum." Said Sean. "Anyone for dessert?" Said Jill happily. "And Mom please?" said LL. "She's a sweaty fleshy pugnacious woman of 78 who claims she's 64 and always has her nose into other people's affairs. She claims roots in The Isle Of Skye but she is descended from the beaker people in Aberdeen, Scotland." Said Sean.

"The generous folds of flesh of a Rubens naked model"... Said Jim forking the last of his clam vogue into his mouth. "Aint going to work on Maggie's farm no more," said Lou. And they all burst out laughing.

After dinner they walked past the boats in the marina and sitting there was a boat with a lit up hot tub steaming in the darkness. Sean said to Jim, "Look Jim someone rich or famous is going for a booze cruise out in the pacific tonight, kind of enticing no." "Unless you're Natalie Wood," Said Lou looking downwards. She spat on the ground and said quietly, "Poor bitch." Her ship had gone off the grid altogether.

They drove back to the bungalow in Santa Rosa. The static was bad tonight it was so dry. Sean said he was going to light a cord in the fireplace for it was a little cold. The rest of them settled down with a glass of red and some mind bending hallucinogenic drugs,some reefer. Jill said, "This is a journey into psychobabble." Sean put on a movie and they all settled down to watch Life Of Brian by the Monty

Python team. The movie, the reefer, the cord, the red wine all added up to an experience of religiosity. An anti-climatically moment of California cleaned lotus-eater repose thought Jim quietly to himself.

Running Wolf was sleeping in a clean bed tonight and for that he felt grateful. He thought about what Kathryn had said to him in the High Street Café later that afternoon. She had said that, "Red Shield would be free to go home in three weeks." He thought about fate and how some people were fated to be born good or evil. He had run into some good people he thought and Running Wolf thought about how he could repay that kindness. Jack was taking him to visit his wife tomorrow.

CHAPTER NINE

The sun dance is a ceremony practiced differently by several North American tribes but several of the ceremonies have features in common, including dancing singing and drumming, the experience of visions, fasting, and in some cases self-torture.

The sun dance was the most spectacular and important religious ceremony of the plains Indians of 19th century North America. Ordinarily held by each tribe once a year usually at the time of the summer solstice.

The Sun Dance lasts from four to eight days starting at the sunset of the final day of preparation and ending at sunset. It showed continuity between life and death A REGENERATION. It shows that there is no true end to life but a cycle of symbolic and true deaths and rebirths. All of nature is intertwined and dependent on one another. This gives an equal ground to everything on earth.

This is similar to the corn king and queen of North East Scotland. For corn in the Quair meant oats to make porridge with or celebrate with a rattle. Or the Celtic Fiefdom, it is a ritual enacted once a year.

Jim and Lou took off for San Francisco the next morning. It was a beautiful sunny day and Lou spotted a blue bird and said to Jim "Look a blue bird over the white cliffs of Dover." Jim replied, "Poetic license, there are no bluebirds in Europe." It was a pretty little thrush and it fluttered off. They were staying one night in Frisco in The Taylor Hotel at Union Square. They said goodbye to Sean and Jill. They really were a lovely couple. Then Lou filled the car with RON 90 leaded gas. They were soon on route 101 for the one hour journey. They tuned in to a radio music station and relaxed into the short journey. They planned to meet up with Jim's friend Karen who worked at Stanford University. She would bless them with her presence. Karen was a musician.

They were soon at the Golden Gate toll bridge. It was not unlike the Forth Road suspension bridge in Scotland although it was longer at about a mile long. Jim found the famous bridge awesome. It was painted international orange. Lou said to Jim, "The engineer John Strauss who designed this bridge was a poet as well so there's hope for you yet guacamole bum." He replied, "The Bridge was opened in 1937 and it is a 20th century masterpiece-it's the second longest bridge in the world. Enough said." Lou came back and said "It has the highest suicide jump rate in the world after Japan, so much for the California dream Babes."

They were soon at the toll and paid their $4 to cross. The toll was for southbound traffic only. When they were on the bridge Jim spotted a vintage white Mercedes convertible heading north, it was immaculate. They would spot a lot more cars like that as they passed over the straits on their way to San Francisco and then LA.

Jim looked across at the city, most of it was built on hills and the wooden buildings were pinky red. Treys gay.

Running Wolf and Cousin Jack took off for the State Mental Hospital in Salem about 11AM. They were meeting Kathryn Morse there at 1PM. It was a two hour journey North on i5. The hospital was set in generous grounds of woodlands, lawns and hedges. As they drove in it began to rain for it was a gray mucky cold day filled with American consciousness. Running Wolf was driving the Black Caddy and he said to Cousin Jack as they arrived at the car park," I like to enjoy four seasons of the year but this year since Red Shield fell ill in the fall I only enjoy three."

The fetid world of the mind, the unwanted those filled with both spiritual and material despair. The BIN.

Cousin Jack replied, "Travel back in time Running Wolf to that safe place before all this began. Trust Kathryn she's a warm seed of truth. Things will look fantastic next spring."

They got out of the car and entered the asylum of fruit and beg. Cousin Jack suddenly thought about a painkiller called VEGANIN he had once picked up in New York and he seriously wondered why it had that name. Kathryn was waiting for them at reception in her goons white coat. They sat down and talked business with her.

She said, "They call Red Shield Adele in here. It's her white name Running Wolf." He looked a little mystified and he faced her off like an animal about to pounce. He had an air of superiority on his face. "Adele means NOBLE in English and she is cured Running Wolf." Said Kathryn. Running Wolf dropped back into him and said, "Who are these people Cousin Jack?"

"We have her on a fortnightly depot shot of Clopixel Decanoate for schizophrenia and she takes an oral medication for mania-carbomazepime every night. She's going to have to take the medication for the rest of her life and she'll never be able to drink or take drugs again. We're going to let her go in three weeks." Said Kathryn.

"Contrary to public opinion they are humanitarians in here, Running Wolf they accept people for who they are," Said Jack. "I'm on medication for the rest of my life, Running Wolf. I'm an alchemist and proud of it." Kathryn said, "You can disagree with white American medicine but noble Adele is dependent on our care."
"YOU" said Kathryn pointedly "Is going to have to look after your wife. Look after her and good things will grow, Salem means secure peace."

It was a howl against the cutting of the wind, the sleet of the angular rain on the buffalo plain where the bison and the black bear lived. The Indian gods summoned Running Wolf to accept that he was not very good at looking after his 30ish wife. That would have to change if he were to have native children suckling on the papoose and continue his line-for there was nothing more ignoble than the end of a family in native America.

Kathryn took them up to the ward. There was the obligatory unlocking and locking of doors. Mesh,

Perspex and full core doors. For it was a secure hospital. As they entered into the bowels of the building they saw patients and nurses rallying up and down the corridor. The patients were allowed to wear civilian clothing and the nurses were wheeling and dealing in white. Many of these patients were being punished for breaking the law. Some of them were murderers, others pedophiles, a bucketful of tongues. The whispered conspiracy of medication and ECT. Deep inside the building they turned left past all the jackrabbits and walked the stairs to Reed Ward where Red Shield was waiting for her husband.

Reed was a name you could trust thought Cousin Jack. It had been 4 months that had shaken Running Wolf's world. Kathryn unlocked the Ward door and all three of them went in. She bolted the door behind her. Running Wolf and Red Shield were desperately in love with each other. There were people young and people not so young on the mixed ward. There was a day room, a kitchen and a smoking room. The Blue Pal TV droned on about the trouble brewing in LA.

They went into the day room and there she was. Adele was sitting opposite the safety amber electric coil fire and the TV wearing a green sweatshirt with California written on the front and dark blue jeans. She wore white espadrilles and her hair was in a ponytail. Her skin was naturally tanned and she had brown hazel eyes. She had been distracted by the Television and the trouble in LA and she was finally so excited to be meeting her husband. She stood up and cuddled and kissed into him, she looked glamorous and she was wearing a wedding ring.

She must have been about 5' 4". Running Wolf said to her, "I think if you pray to the gods, Adele, you will have love in your life. Through the night it will be the beginning of a wonderful relationship." Adele said to anyone who was listening, "Things are going well, I have a husband who loves me."

A man who is over 5 feet tall and has a scar and a driving license is someone worth holding on to. They all sat down and Kathryn said they could have a coffee. She said to Cousin Jack he could go into the smoke hole and have a cigarette if he wanted to. Running Wolf wanted some time on his own with his wife so he could tell her how he had been doing. Adele said to her husband, "You enter into a certain mindset when you come into this place I am still here and for that I have to thank the patience and love of the nurses and the doctors." Running Wolf said, "This has changed all my priorities you being in here I thought they used hypnosis and that the drugs gave you the heebeegeebees. But I was wrong I have turned my grief into something positive, Red Shield."

Kathryn had gone to the nurse's station and left them alone. They began to talk in Crow and Jack couldn't talk he felt like crying. He went to the smoke hole so they could have some time alone and he wasn't a novice in places like this. He helped himself to a white coffee in the kitchen. There was one patient in the smoke hole.

He was dressed in jackboots, army camouflage trousers, jacket and cap and introduced himself as Gavin Rockwell with a, "Hiya." His head was shaved completely bald and he was smoking rolling tobacco and a packet of Drum and a packet of JOB papers lay beside the ashtray. He had china blue eyes and looked like a cloned pig. There was a stifling acrid smell of smoke under the ubiquitous strip light overhead. The last of the gray day shone through the meshed Perspex window. Cousin Jack sat down opposite him on one of the varnished blonde wood and orange vinyl chairs.

He lit up an Old Gold and tossed the half open packet beside the ashtray. He took a draw, a slurp of his coffee and looked at Rockwell. He virtually had no teeth. He had four bottom teeth and one upper tusk only. What a fucking dangerous looking binger thought Jack. He could tell that Rockwell was a neofascist and a white supremacist. He was one of those people that omitted to ever realize that on the whole all you pass on to your children is love. Rockwell was one of those people that thought there was only one thing you passed on to your offspring and that was your blood.

Rockwell said, "I could fairly use a drink I haven't had a drink for three months." "Well don't look at me buster," said Jack "I can't break you out and I'm not going to buy drink for you even if you did have any money. What are you in for," Said Jack to the psychotic monster. "I stabbed a Jew in a bar in Newport and I'm in here without limit of time." Jack wasn't very intimidated by his madness and said, "I can see you doing some serious soul searching in here Gavin." Rockwell had all the maturity and the gums to match of a two year old and he said, "I'll put a spell on you, I can't stand it coz your fine and I'm not. Get to fuck" Cousin Jack was the moral compass of the ward and he said," I had sex with a woman yesterday and I don't have to pay for it so you had better shut your mouth or I'll knock what's left of your teeth down your throat." That fairly shut him up for the remainder of Cousin Jack's cigarette for Rockwell wasn't so brave without a drink inside him. Jack picked up his cigarettes and went and rejoined Running Wolf and Adele.

Norman had been up all night in the house in Leverburgh South West Harris. He sat by the phone waiting for Jim's grandmother Nora Cumming to phone. Peace and quiet he was tormented with the dreams of his incomplete life. Kirsty his young home help would be here in an hour, an excuse to have another whisky with her.

He had spoken to his second GP Roddy Ross in Bournemouth last night. Roddy had always stood by Norman, through the back street abortions, The bar fights, the lung cancer. For Roddy had parachuted into Arnhem, A Bridge To Far.

He was sending him a script for Valium 10s' to help him get his head down.

Jim hadn't phoned him-he thought he was a cack-handed young man For Norman. DADA had always had a temperamental relationship with his sons. He needed them now and there was always the question of his bastard Kenyan son Magnus in Paisley. That Buddy had spared him a crime. For Norman had led a full careless life and now he was paying the price. The thoughts, the thoughts that kept him awake all night like Harpies on the North Atlantic wind.

The Queen had commissioned him in 1954 and he

had served with the GLORIOUS GLOSTERS. One cap badge to the front one to the rear devil get thee ahint me. And now? It was of no importance mere watermarks on bonded paper.

The fire lay cold and dead in the grate. Kirsty would be determined to light the fire and set him in warm west coast spirits with sprite and chat. There was always his good Episcopalian neighbors Pat and Jack at number 6 The Terrace. They were tea planters and merely frowned at Norman's dubious taste for company. "Dash it," he thought to himself I commanded a platoon in Korea. They and Donald Norman the fisher of men's souls supported people in their community.

Norman lit a fresh Silk Cut purple and finished the last of his whisky. He had drunk a bottle of BELLABEG COOKING last night and yet he had drunk himself sober. The phone rang and his loneliness caused him to pounce on the receiver like an eagle.

"Hello," he said in best RP English for Norman had been educated at The Edinburgh Academy, The Nicholson Institute and Edinburgh University. He had needed careful handling for he was unusually talented. That careful handling he had not received from his Victorian father. Magnus the Paisley Buddy had flourished since his arrival in Scotland on a visa. He was a drug Lord and dealt in crack cocaine and dirty money. But two years in jail and a depuration order lay waiting in the wings for him. The Queen had seen to that for her family had stubbornly and subtly always supported the Cumming Clan.

Ian had seen his time during the first world war spent on the Italian front for in the Royal Artillery he would not have survived the Somme, Paschendale, Mons or even the Ypres salient. King George the 5th had sensibly seen to his survival as Queen Elizabeth the 2nd had seen to Norman trying to get it right.

"Hello Ducky its Mama here."
"Hello Mama Comarahaile"
"I'm fine Nono how are you?"
"Oh not so great I feel dashed lonely" (more indications of self-pity)
"Kirsty will be in today wont she Bettie McClelland comes to see me this morning."
"Oh Mama I am so pleased that Bettie will be with you today."
"If only Betsy Caird were with you Nono I wouldn't worry about you so much, if only you hadn't lost your mate."
"She's the love of my life I guessed tonight isn't my lucky night". . .
Norman was so hen pecked by his mother that it left him confined like a little boy. For he was Peter Pan after all. He had been a foolish fellow and now Kirsty was his Tinkerbell.
"Has James phoned you yet I haven't heard from him?"
"He has phoned Betsy he's having a great time as you know."
Those made Norman feel a little better for if the truth were known his children were of peripheral interest and at the core of his life lay his relationship with his strong Louisiana schist Lewis mother in Edinburgh.

"Lisa as I like to think of her is the last plant to flower." Said Nora. "The window of a Hebridean

Summer is brief Norman They're young they are enjoying themselves."
"The wild harvest is under way if I know Jim."
Nora let out a cackle for her experiences on The Gold Coast in Africa had left her a woman with a broad mind.
"I'll ring you tonight Mama it's my turn I'll phone after Coronation Street."
"Okay Norman, take care, Goodbye."
"Goodbye Mama." And they both put the phone down.

Cousin Jack and Running Wolf had taken up stations in The High Street Café at 10pm and now it was closing time, time to go home. Red Shield was being discharged on the 25th in the morning. Running Wolf would go to Salem and pick her up. When they were in Salem after the mental hospital they went to visit an old couple called Roger and Bonnie Hull, he was a retired Professor of Art and Jack knew their motorcycling son well. Jack had been astounded that in conversation Roger had not even heard of the "Two Roberts". They were the two most important post war artists to have emerged from Scotland. They had been part of the Soho Bohemia scene. They were a mystery to Roger Hull and Jack sometimes felt ashamed that there was such cultural ignorance amongst the so called intelligentsia of West Coast America. Whatever floats your upturned boat for Jim would do well here. Perhaps all America was fit for was Jackson Pollock's spatial craps or Mark Rothko's boring abstractions. Jim would do well here for it did not take that much to succeed in America. Just hard work and diligence.

Jack took a draught of his Jaffrey's and said to Running Wolf, "Will you go back to the Reservation straight away or will you stay, there is a job with me." Running Wolf replied, "I am the eldest of a big family I must return and look after my people they are the most important people to me. Red Shield has forced me to realize that." "Well you're the man," Said Jack reflectively. "Let me have a party for you up in The Blue Moon in Portland to welcome Red Shield home, it will just be a small intimate gathering then we can all move on. It is what I do-entertaining, Running Wolf." "Okay, Jack, Adele would like that." Jack was a real special guy he was the leader of a tight knit family. He had put himself on the line for Running Wolf and Running Wolf was flourishing since he had run into Lou. He was about to realize his full potential as a clan chief and warrior.

Lou and Jim had spent the night with Karen she was an Afro Caribbean princess from Glasgow and she worked in the Musical Education Dept. at Stanford. They had gone for a meal in a fish restaurant that night and Jim had a gay guy making eyes at him. Karen and Lou had thought it was hysterical over the Guinness and clams and Jim had given him the victory 'Vs.' San Francisco had been the gay capital of the world until AIDS and SARS had devastated the bathhouses. San Francisco was cautiously conservative in its cultural scene and it had changed a great deal since it had been the staging post for the journey of On The Road. They had visited Height Asbury in the afternoon and the blaze of the hippy trip in the late sixties had been replaced with . . . well nothing. Just Jakes pushing shopping carts. In a tic Lou had realized that in America things had deteriorated considerably since she had been away.

Conservatism had replaced democracy with the violent aspirations of Middle Eastern Liberty. For the road to hell was filled with America's good intentions. The Beagle of the world was no longer a benign watchdog but was perceived as the imperialist aggressor.

It was a presidential election year in America and the country was tired for change. If Bill Clinton were elected it would remain to be seen whether he would make a positive difference or if he would turn out to be yet another Gubernatorial sleaze ball. Lou had read a lot about the saxophone playing Arkansas Governor and she had thought that if he were elected he would bring peace to Northern Ireland for he was of Irish descent. Whether he would bring any Eastern promise was another matter altogether.

Karen had two boyfriends one was a yard from Puerto Rico who sat on her bed and smoked green and the other was a Texan psychedelic water engineer (plumber) called Ram. She didn't have much time for either of them for she had had her heart broken by Ian Slater a Macedonian musician. She didn't so much suffer from hardening of the arteries as a well developed halo that was a very good judge of character.

Carla had visited the Belmont hospital it had been confirmed that she had a shadow on her left lung. She was to start radiotherapy right away but she was going to be all right. They had managed to catch the tumor in time and a small biopsy proved it wasn't malignant. She and Mannie Kennedy was an item now. And she had given up drug dealing. She stopped smoking right away and no longer went near dope.

For Banes means ready and willing and it was the bean found in the last portion of Twelfth Night cake baked by LL. She was Show.

Billy Patterson still mooched about her and they were determined to shite on Cousin Jack on the 25th of January. But that set up would prove to be a disaster. Billy Patterson now had Carla's business and there was no stopping him now. He continued to sell MDMA cut with hexamine. There had been a spate of flat liners and deaths associated with this particular nasty batch and the police were concerned. Billy Patterson had never seen Carla look so alive for she was a lovely looking bird. There were vertical rainbows coming from Carla's apartment now that she had the love of a good man for Mannie Kennedy was a man of simple tastes. She had even managed to lose some weight from her bum. It had to be said though that Carla was jealous of Cousin Jack and she had always tried to see what was in it for him in her relationship with him. It was a mark of true friendship if you met someone's family and Jack had never met any of Carla's family except her brother who was a cosmetic breast surgeon in LA.

She had been a guest at Cousin Jack's failed disastrous marriage to Sandra Knight when they had got married in THE WATER OF LIFE bar in Portland some 23 years ago when Portland Maid of Honor was the Danish Shipping magnate Valetta Mares McKinney Arleen. Who was conservatively the richest woman in the world? Cousin Jack was very close to Valetta for she had always looked out for him when he had got himself into scrapes. Some sunny day Jack was really gone for Sandra had a lesbian affair with Valetta, although it was true to say that Jack had also had an affair with Valetta who was an adopted Texan and lived in Dallas. At the wedding night later on Carla who had offered herself up on a plate (for she was always looking for, a brighter place to rest her little heap) had plagued Valetta. Oil was Valetta's forte for the Mares refineries and their seven-pointed star were poised to well supply the markets in Europe with crude oil. Crude? Valetta was a fine born aristocratic girl who was at the top of her game and the oil refineries merely proved a distraction for her considerable shipping acumen for she was the little mermaid of Copenhagen and there was nothing she enjoyed more than cold water scuba diving. Indeed Valetta had become pregnant with a baby boy called Caleb and it had been widely thought that the real father of her boy was Cousin Jack and not her husband the BEAT Poet Charles Bukowski.

Lou and Jim left San Francisco the next day and drove down to San Luis Obispo. It was bear country and also home of the symbiotic children. A place so raven by eugenics that all the young beautiful people who stalked the streets emptily had an average IQ of about 76 and were like character's from the Henrik Ibsen play Ghosts. It was a strange place to say the least and Jim found it hysterical to see all these sunny blue-eyed Ken and Barbie dolls of children that inhabited the place. To say there was an overdose of workhouse eugenics was a gross understatement. Jim said to Lou in the morning in the motel, "Let's get the hell out of dodge Louise." They beat it. In the car Lou thought out aloud and said to Jim, "You're going to like LA Jim it's weird like Aberdeen". . .

After breakfast of chocolate dough rings and white coffee at Winchells Lou put on some Calvin Klein obsession,Jude had bought her some for Christmas and it was all the rage just now. It was a pungent cloying odor and Jim was reminded of the time just before he met Lou in Glasgow when he was working as the engineer for The Coats Viyella wool coy façade retention contract in 279 St. Vincent Street Glasgow. It was a dangerous exhausting contract and falling on the site had almost killed Jim. On the Saturday of the Orange Walk he had been working and the catholic laborers on the site made them scarce when part of the parade went past. If Jim in his North East naiveté had crossed the march he would have been beaten up,as it was he was content to just watch. Such was the strength of religious bigotry in Glasgow where people used knives and threw bricks and bottles. That night he had dreamt that the man Jimmy Boyle in The Griffin bar in Glasgow had slashed him once. He had also dreamt of Louise and they were driving through a wheat field. It was a momentary dream but a powerful one where he had visited the boutiques in LA. And then he met the woman of his dreams.

As they sat outside Winchells he said to Lou in a tic, "Remember when I worked at Coats Viyella Lou in Glasgow, when we met I mean." "Yes," said Lou." It was return of the native you went back to your trade in the summer months when you were at University and that site was a particularly dangerous one. It was a Private Finance Initiative contract and there was no Clerk of Works on the job. More Thatcher folly-the irresponsible bitch." "Well," said Jim, "I found this old leather suitcase that had been bricked up in one of the basement catacombs and inside the suitcase was a plan of the Cabbage Patch plot in Leslie Fife. It reminded me, Lou, of The Kailyard Artists in Scotland." "I reckon that was a set up Jim, it had been left there by your old pal Ryan O Neal so that you would be reminded of the time when you were a little boy in Leslie and he stole a cake from your Mom's window sill and got you all through when your father Norman turned out to be a drunkard. He just hid the suitcase there to get you interested in real concrete writing and real money unlike JM Barrie and Peter Pan, and lead you to your final destination with me and also being a Beat poet and a writer. For Ryan O Neal once stole your bike and left an old French bike in its place so that you would cry and get mad and interested in cycling. You did and became National Team Champion. For you have been "in" since 1973 when you peaked at Mile-End primary school." Said Lou. And you met your French speaker-non?" said Lou brightly. "Oui Oui," replied Jim.

They were making for Ventura in Ventura County where they were staying that night with Lou's favorite former high school teacher Chris Guthrie and his wife Jolene from Omaha Nebraska. As Lou and Jim drove down route 101 Jim said to Lou, "Chris Guthrie is some name for that is the heroine of Sunset Song." "He doesn't make anything of his Scottish roots I doubt if he has ever heard of Leslie Mitchell and A SCOTS QUAIR. It is compulsory reading for any writer for it describes the sheer folly of The Great War. It is a symbolic true novel." Said Lou. My grandfather Jim from Angus had horses, working horses, Clydesdales. All my people on my mother's fathers side were farm servants from the Mearns, and all my people on my father's father side started out as farm servants in Fife." Said Jim. "I know you love the countryside Jim and would be happier settling in a village somewhere but if we make it we can be the TWO siblings in Italo Calvino's novel,the town mouse and the country mouse. You are a MAKAR Jim. You are ready now, to work and find your voice now that you have found your soul mate."

They made good progress and at rush hour found themselves North of Ventura. Shisholop-originally the home of the Chumash Indians. It was Spanish in it's influence and was home of the world's largest organization of citrus growers and there was also oil there. The Santa Ana winds were blowing and they could taste the rain salt. Soon they were on the Ventura freeway and making for Chris and Jolene's. Just South of Santa Barbara. Lloyd Cole and the Commotions came on the radio and the red lights of the cars tailgating on the freeway reminded Lou and Jim of Glasgow University, Prince El Gamal and Otago Street, It was dusk and they were in Southern California. The wind drag buffeted the car and Lou said they should get the couple a bottle of wine. They pulled into Safeway's at Nickel's canyon and bought a bottle of Californian champagne, which was made with the method champenois. Lou said it was slightly sweeter than European champagne for California accounted for over 90% of American wine production and the American palate was slightly sweeter. Lou and Jim held hands in the car park of Safeway's. Lou was wearing her sun bleached cut off Levi's and Jim could make out the shape of her wonderful vagina underneath. She was getting a tan and her legs were supple and athletic. "Me and You just singing in the park just waiting in the dark," sang Lou.

Lou sparked up a joint in the car for Jill had given her a marijuana reefer. They smoked it in the car park and felt at once just in love again. For Jim when he had met Lou had thrown a wine glass against the wall and had said to her with Soul II Soul playing, "To the very end."

They arrived at Chris and Jolene's an hour later. The house was stucco facade and had an orange tree growing in the hacienda. Chris was delighted to see his star pupil again and embraced her and said, "It's the woman in the red bikini." For Lou was a strong swimmer and swimming had got her through the long Scottish winters. Chris was about 6" with sandy hair and sea green eyes. Jolene was in the open plan chaparral kitchen preparing beef tacos; salad and she got some Tecate brews from the large refrigerator. She said, "Hi Lou and Jim when you get drunk between the moon and New York city the best that you can do is fall in love . . . have a beer and make yourselves at home." They went through to the living room, which was one step down from the open plan kitchen. It was warm citrus colors. A parrot squawked in its cage "Hi Daddy." Chris said, "Don't pay any attention to her Jim that's Cindy. She's a peach face love bird."

Lou and Jim sat down. The TV was on and things in LA were heating up in South Central there had been a lot of arrests. Chris said, "Don't worry about the blacks stoning the cops that's a long way off." He switched off the television for he preferred the radio and was a VHF radio ham. Lou said we'll be there tomorrow Chris I'm in love with an old fashioned man all he wants to do is play guitar and sing and I'm just as broke as a girl could be." Jim looked at his wife tenderly and took her hand. Jim said that is enough of your romanticizing rambling Lou we'll soon be in Mexico." And LA would seem a long way away. Jolene came through from the kitchen and sat down, she was about 50 and had red brown hair and wore glasses. They had decided as a couple not to have children and they were consistently content with one another and their talking parrot Cindy. She squawked, "Hi Mom."

Jolene took a drink of her Tecate and said, "Make it one for my baby and one more for the road."

They ate at around eight in the breakfast bar. Lou and Jim were both tired after their long drive, you never got enough sleep when you were traveling sleep was at a premium. Chris said over dinner "There are a hell of a lot more down and outs on the road between here and LA than when you were last here Lou. Most of them have an alcohol or drugs problem, the drug of choice is heroin." Lou replied, "If you are going to be poor this is the place to be poor for it has a Mediterranean climate and there is food growing everywhere. You should see it in Glasgow and Aberdeen back in Scotland,that's real depravity." Said Lou. "I help out at an American Red Cross shelter with Jolene two nights a week,it's more like a transit camp with everyone heading north." said Chris. He added, "If you are black you may as well not show." Lou added, "And the all-white jury agreed." She told Chris and Jolene about the old warrior Running Wolf. They were all agreed that he had had a lucky escape with Louise's help. Everything for him was going to be all right although his wife was still going to require therapy as an outpatient up in Oregon.

Jim said, "Increasingly there is large groups of people on the move just now. Europe is no different for apart from the Pictish tribes in North East of Scotland the rest of the country except for the predominantly island Celtics, (No-one knows where the Hebrideans came from for Gaelic was a non Indo European language ancient whale bones), is an Arboretum with groups of people-a nation of immigrants-standing apart. It is not indigenous. My family originally was from the Middle East and obscurely turned up in France during the dark ages and arrived in Scotland as part of the Norman Conquest." You are a Pict Chris the Guthrie's are from Angus north of Dundee." "My family are Polish," said Jolene," I can still make a mean chitterling soup; my grin taught me the recipe." Lou smiled and took a drink of her Tecate. She looked at Jim and said proudly, "My husband lost his virginity to a Polish Aristocrat Angie Okroj. Angel dust." "We all have to learn to write and ride a bike sometime" Said Jolene happily. There was the noise of dogs fighting outside. Chris said, "Don't worry about that Southern Ca. is as bad as Greece for wild dogs although there isn't any rabies." "Just a nasty bite," said Jolene."

"Do you think Chris that the Victorians were right and that charity begins at home?" Said Lou playing Devil's Advocate. "Well there hasn't been much of a home in America since the 50s'. When technology saw all the people living in a subterranean suburban world driving Buick's and living well in California because of the Hoover Dam. And all the men were having affairs with the secretary it anticipated JFK and Camelot. "Said Chris. "At least he didn't take it out on the American people he may have behaved monstrously towards women but he didn't deserve to be assassinated for that." Said Jolene. "Ha ha, Most American people the lower middle classes are a long way from home the place you want to be all the time "Herewith" said Jim.

"I have met quite a few of the valley girls said Lou that is wrong. California should be about Mannie Steinbeck and the land of plenty milk and honey. But if you aint got no doh Rae me," Said Lou, "You might as well leave the Garden of Eden." She added.

"Do you really think Faith has much currency in the valley of the Dolls?"

Most of Those kids just take and go to their latest Hollywood prom they have no respect for the peasant pride of the mid westerners who built California into the bountiful place it is today." Said Chris angrily. "Both Jolene and I are educators-teachers of English." Jim said, "In Scotland happy valleys are Valium tens' and Belair is a hairspray to get high on. When the musician Sheena Easton returns to Glasgow and Bellshill she is lucky to escape with her life for that is how bitter Urban Scotland's smile is."

"The writer to watch out for in Scotland is Irvine Welsh," Said Jim, "He really has captured the voiceless nest of urban Scotland. In one of his short stories A FAULT ON THE LINE he describes the results of kids playing around on the railroad line someone gets squashed to death and all that happens is the train is delayed briefly a total teenage wasteland and what is more he writes in the urban lowland vernacular."

"Yeah that is quite a feat-Joyce was able to pull off the urban vernacular in Ulysses and the contemporary Dublin scene. That is why you were such a good pupil Lou you were interested in English Literature." Said Chris. "My favorite writer when I was in your class Chris was Ambrose Bierce. I think the Coup De Grace is just about the best short story ever written." Said Louise Lisa. "He was one of the great American writers," said Jolene, "He was as talented as Sherwood Anderson or Mark Twain a biting critic and satirist but ultimately he proved to be so self destructive he died in mysterious circumstances during the Mexican Revolution in 1913.

"And you're going to Mexico," said Chris, "Hasta la vista baby."

Cousin Jack woke up in his house next to the High Street Café at 8AM. He had gone to bed at 11PM the previous night and had listened to the Radio.The BBC World Service. He was wearing boxer shorts and was otherwise naked. He went into the kitchen and poured himself some orange Juice and took his morning medication. He was type2 diabetic and also had suffered from Schizoid Affective Disorder. He hadn't had a manic episode for 35 years. His hair was electric stasis and he smoothed it down with his hands. He had on his Bally mules. His medication was in a weekly blister pack so it was easy to ensure that he always took the right medication. He had started a vicious chest cold and the cold had laid its ghost upon his lungs and he had a terrible cough and a running nose. He lit up a cigarette and fed his black and white bibbed cat Ike some cat food. Jack also was on antibiotic, multi vitamins, iron, a cherry linctuses cough bottle and paracetemol. He said to the cat, "Eat up little baby you need your strength." He then went back into his bedroom and sat on the edge of the bed. He lit up an old gold. He said to himself, "One of the aspects of being an entertainer is that you get these vivid dreams of all souls of the world cramming in your subconscious mind." And after Jack drank some more orange juice he had just about stuttered awake. He had had a dream about his Late Mother Ethel in the early morning. Ethel had offered him a tasty codfish to eat an east coast fish. He took it as a lucky omen for he had never dreamt that he would meet Jacks so late in life.

Jack opened the curtains it had been raining and the asphalt in the high street was shiny in the morning sunshine. He went to the sink and ran the hot water he was going to have a hot shave and the water ran cold, tepid then warm. He plugged the sink and washed his face. With hypoallergenic soap. He then placed the razor in the water. He looked in the mirror. He then ran the water again until in a tic it was hot. He smoothed the pine nut barbasol onto his face and shaved himself. After shaving he toweled his face dry and looked at his star eyes in the mirror- they were windows to such an old soul. He then put on his dressing gown and went back into the kitchen. Ike had eaten his food and Jack let him out the side Kitchen door into the garden. He briefly looked at the apple tree, it was gnarled and old and was in outspread supplication to the gods. He then went and made himself some porridge, coffee, bacon and eggs for breakfast. Running Wolf would be through soon. He would do his American Navy exercises after breakfast before he showered and got dressed and faced the day.

Lou and Jim took off early in the morning for LA. Lou had given Chris her copy of a Scots Quair so Chris could discover something about his own identity he had been really touched and when he thanked her his sea green eyes were misty.

They headed onto the Ventura Freeway. Lou was driving and she was an old pro in Los Angeles. Soon they were in the San Fernando Valley. A whole population of cherry linctuses. It was already warm at 7AM and the flat roofed wooden villas stood out on the edges of the six lane concrete freeway. There was ballast on their roofs to keep the tar flat. Pretty soon they were caught up in traffic and Lou said, "They say to keep your eyes straight ahead here and not look around at the other drivers if you want to avoid a drive by. But me I like to look at the Angelinos." She thought of the many Hispanics and Mexicans in LA. The Angelitos were the little children that had died and they were celebrated in The Mexican Day Of the Dead on 31st October. Sleep. It was a Mexican public holiday and the mother's and fathers of the perished little children would leave flowers and effigies at the roadside. For Mexican culture fundamentally believed in rebirth.

Pretty quickly the traffic was on the move and the LA smog from the freeway did it's best to obscure the disc of the sun. Jim liked the rough palling smell of

American gas. At Sherman Oaks they took the turning for the San Diego Freeway drove through Brentwood and turned onto the Santa Monica freeway. They were heading for the beach at Santa Monica. They went down through Santa Monica to the boardwalk where they parked up. It was 10AM. Lou had on her Levi cut offs and a red bikini top. The public beach of the pacific was almost deserted except for dog walkers. They sat down beside a Japanese Angelino who was reading Sons And Lovers by DH Lawrence. She was wearing a white bikini and was very sexy. Lou said, "There is a lot more sex here in LA than up in Portland. That girl has had more different rides than a used horse's collar, you can tell." Lou had on her LA bullshit detector and as if to prove her point a sand fly landed on the girl's crotch. They sat for a while talked, drank a coke and smoked. They then went back to the car for Jim was expecting them at 12AM. Jim noticed the beachfront apartments, they was the homes of Artists and musicians and at once Jim was seduced by LA for rents were cheap. It had a Mediterranean climate and was on the pacific rim of the western world.

They got onto the Santa Monica freeway and drove the short drive to West Hollywood and Sunset Strip. Jim was taken with the architecture. There were fantastic and elaborate apartment buildings from Hollywood's golden age. An architectural giggle of extreme Art Deco, Spanish colonial revival, Monterey Revival, Italianate monsters and fountains and statues, hidden gardens and ironwork and detailing.

Then suddenly they were at Jimmy's little stucco

facade apartment amongst the palm trees of Swail Drive. They parked up with the car pointed in the same direction as oncoming traffic. They went in and rang the bell of his apartment. It was fragile frayed sunny which was accentuated by the organicity of the white that was everywhere.

Jimmy answered them and he buzzed them up. Jim had encountered the Edinburgh bohemian scene where he had stayed up all night to be let into his Brother's apartment in the morning by his first serious girlfriend the artist Lisa Morocco. She was now LA and Jim had briefly thought she was going to become his sister in law. "This is an Arts Community like the Abbey," said Lou. As she heard the sound of someone playing the trombone, a booming neighbor she realized that this was where she and Jim would eventually come for neither of him or her could stand the winter further North not to mention the brutal Scottish winters. "It is wonderful if you contribute," Said Lou. What did Jimmy have to offer thought Jim for he was a poor soul. They went in. The lobby was Art Deco white with ornamental electric lights at either side of the staircase. They walked up the staircase to jimmy's little apartment. He welcomed them in. He had been at work in the morning and he was ratty for he had the gun but no ammunition to put in it. His apartment consisted of a large bed sitting room, a dressing room, a kitchen and a bathroom. Jim noticed the medium height ceilings had been artexed with quartz stone so it shone starkly in the light. Lou had brought up their skyline bag and Jim had the sleeping bags. Jimmy said, "Dump it in the dressing room that is where you are sleeping tonight." It was tiny and filled with Jimmy's American clothes and patent leather shoes.

Jimmy had one picture on hi wall a picture of Freddie Mercury for he was a gay icon. "The good news Jimmy is that we are staying for one night so you can moan about anything you like bros." Said Lou. Jim had picked up four cans of Coors from the local Italian delicatessen. They had had bagels with cream cheese and jam for a brunch and the people in the store had been really friendly towards the arty young couple when they had seen the Ecosse sticker on the back of the Toyota. Jim put the mustard colored Coors in the empty refrigerator and went and took a piss. He noticed the sun streaking in the window for yellow is the color of sunshine. Jim realized that Hollywood was a slice of water scarce paradise an oasis.

Jim came back through Jimmy was sitting on the couch and he was snorting cocaine. Jim said, "Oyo you don't do that in front of my wife." Jimmy was non-plussed and put away his little silver coke spoon and dollar bill. Jimmy was a cocaine addict more or less for he found reality hard to cope with. For he was not bullet proof and could not run with the tigers. He was an in-between. It was quite a performance thought Lou and plus he wouldn't have cared if he was on a class A drug in front of my man.

"We are going to Aunt Hopes in Glendale tonight for dinner do you want to come Jimmy?" Said Lou. "Nah," said Jimmy, "I'm going out tonight. I'll get pizza." Jim suddenly realized that Jimmy was as cynical as an acid burn he had reverted to the LA sociopath and wasn't interested in Lou and Jim or family. For it was an innate thing because he was a misfit. He had nothing to reveal. Lou hoped he wasn't about to have a moan in.

"We are going out," said Lou "Can we have your spare key?" Jimmy got them his spare key. He said, "Don't lose it little sis." Lou wouldn't lose it for she had the lot.

Jim and Lou left the apartment and decided to take the short walk up Wiltshire Boulevard to Rodeo Drive. It was a short fourblock drive and had the most sought after stores including Louis Vuitton, Chanel, Hermes, Burberry and Coach. This sort of boutique shopping was of little interest to a beat class couple like Jim and Lou for if someone sold you a car they wouldn't care if you never drove it. Jim noticed the Moroccan embassy was on Rodeo. Little did he know that Jacks was French Moroccan on her mother's side? She really was the most exotic demonian on the planet. They went into an art gallery and had a look at the paintings. Jim wondered if the moaner of the week ever came up here? They went and got a couple of skinny Lattes then returned to Jimmy's apartment. He wasn't in and he had drunk two of Jim's Coors. Lou turned on the radio,it was an LA pop station that was playing non-stop eighties dance tracks.

They both relaxed on Jimmy's bed settee and listened to the radio. Lou said to Jim, "What's your favorite color Jim?" He looked at the starry ceiling and said, "The color of your eyes Lou it's hard to pin down. It's very sexy you know, very exotic." "What's your favorite color Louise?" said Jim. "I have two favorite colors chocolate and white." Jim said, "See the face you love light up with Terrys All Gold. Fancy a Rolo?" "Please Jim," and he popped one in her mouth.

Jim felt like a little rumpy pumpy but Lou said, "No It's Jimmy he could be back anytime. It's getting dark it's time to go over to Hope's we'll have to stop for gas." "Okay," said Jim dutifully. "Hope makes a mean martini." Said Lou.

They got ready to go out. Lou changed into a black skirt and a midnight blue tee shirt. She cleaned her face with alcohol and cotton pads. They had done

Jim spoke to the shopkeeper briefly after buying the wine, he seemed shaken up as the noise of a police siren wah-wahed in the near distance. He said to Jim, "You're Scots are you?" Jim said "Yeah" and the young first generation European said he was a Lithuanian Jew; he shook Jim's hand although he was living on the edge of a war-zone. Jim intuited by his eyes what he was thinking, He said, "You left Lithuania for this". . . Shot by both sides for what he had left behind was no better. The Jew let the comment hang in the air and said in a Lithuanian accent, as if searching for succor, as if searching for recognition, "You have a nice evening now, take care." Jim went back tensely to the car where Lou was filling up the windshield bottle with water and was checking the oil. "Everything's cool," she said, and they took off onto Sunset Boulevard towards the Griffith observatory, Burbank then Glendale.

Norman had known the men of Glendale for it was named after the small in terms of population but large in terms of territory community in North West Skye. Jim also had known the men of Glendale for he had been Site Engineer on a Sewerage Scheme in Dunvegan 4 miles South of Glendale. This was the distance they were faced urbanely with now. Murdo Macleod the laborer had been one of the nicest men he had met in his short life. He worked as a laborer and kept a croft as well. It was the family croft in Glendale and he spoke Gaelic as his first language. He kept a couple of Kye and grew a little oats. He was honest. Donnie Mackenzie had chosen him for the contract in Dunvegan. Jim had stayed in THE MAN'S HOTEL in Dunvegan. The hotel was the Misty Isle and THE MAN from Glendale was Alex Morrison the boxing promoter. He had promoted Mike Tyson and knew Don King well. As it was Mannie Patrick Jim's brother had worked in The Misty Isle when it had been owned by Alex Ross one of the men of Glendale part of a family of thirteen. For Norman had married the widow of James Ross (Elizabeth) the famous Gaelic scholar and brother to Alex and Roddy Ross. Alex had sold the hotel and bar to Alex Morrison.

James had been a major in the Chindits in Burma in WWII and died in a mysterious car accident outside Glasgow on the M8 in 1973 when his brother Roddy had been driving. James had been decapitated. Wild is the wind-where the women are strong and the men are good looking. The men of Glendale.

They made their way down the Sunset Strip heading North East towards Glendale California. The atmosphere on the strip was intimidating for men were fighting and being simultaneously shaken down by the police everywhere on the sidewalks both left and right. Jim was reminded of one time he had driven through Paisley once on a Saturday night-another war zone.

The cars of the city go rushing by. Downtown the bright lights. "You know life is cruel Jim Keep staring ahead." Said Lou. "Oh don't try to stop baby hold me tight, we are the kids in America." Replied Jim. It was all like a bad case of flu like death warmed up. How do you get rid of and through white medieval hate thought Jim. These men don't buy rounds-they would drink you dry of the roots of the maltlets. Single rare malt like the ANTIQUARY.

Soon enough they had turned left off the Strip and it was over-they had given it the slip. In a tic Lou lit up an Old Gold and exhaled in relief like a sleep driving angel. She said, "The sun never shined on me until that left turn came around." That is a serious derailment of law and order," replied Jim, "People are dying needlessly tonight Lou." "Try walking," said Lou. "It makes you think twice before taking to the Strip on a Friday night," replied Jim. Pretty soon they were driving North West through Burbank the industrial end of the film Industry and Jim was reminded of Denmore Road, the slick oil industry estate in the Bridge of Don in Aberdeen. The home of Brown & Root. The lonely existential dark dank driving image under the high overhead lights would be graven on his soul the rest of his life.

Soon they were in Glendale and parking outside Hope's on a steep hill.

The Jewel City.

They went into Hope's apartment. Hope looked like Judith and wore glasses, she was an American

JACK NICHOLSON

beauty like Annette Benning and her eyes were the same blue green as Lou's. Jim handed over the wine and Hope was genuinely touched by this young Highland Scotsman's thoughtfulness. "Well thank you Jim welcome to my small home." Said Hope. She had retired some fifteen years ago from Tiffany's and her constant companion now was her American shorthair cat Smokey. Hope reminded Jim of his great aunt Jess who had led a life and was now fiercely independent in her small apartment in Torry. Lou said to Hope, "I'll pour us all a Martini I think Jim could do with something to stiffen his resolve."

I heard that there is trouble downtown in LA on the radio tonight. Hope said, she added, "Don't you ever be scared of ridicule Jim you are a prince and your Lou is the luckiest girl in America. Let's have a drink before we break bread." Hope had a smoking leather purse and pulled out a Virginia slim and lit herself up and sat down.

Jim was struck by the antediluvian quaintness of the apartment,the phone was dial up and there were shiny plastic covers to protect the upholstery of cat's hairs. Hope had made Martini's and Lou poured out three glasses of vodka Martini's from the iced cocktail shaker.

Lou and Jim could make themselves at home here for they were filled with hope. The cocktails tasted sophisticated and American,the stuff of full social calendars.

They had two cocktails before dinner and Lou asked her aunt about Tiffany's. "Well Lou I worked at the store in the corner of 5th Avenue and 37th street in Manhattan I was a buyer." Said Hope. "The store was a location for the movie Breakfast at Tiffany's. Starring your gorgeous double Audrey Hepburn. The Tiffany diamond is the yellow diamond, which is on display in the New York store. The Astors and the Vanderbilt's wore Tiffany's diamonds and Tiffany's blue book catalog is the yardstick for all other Jewelry stores. Tiffany's doesn't buy back diamonds unlike other retail stores. Tiffany's doesn't just sell jewelry it sells silver platinum and gold jewelry and also china. Recently Tiffany's branched out into perfume." Lou said to Hope "Do you like my opal ear studs Jim bought them for me in Scotland. "They are probably Australian by origin because 95% of Opals are from Australia." Said Hope. "The story goes that the Aborigines believed the creator came down to earth spreading peace and where he touched earth it sparkled with opals . . . in the colors of the rainbow." Added Hope. "These ones are a subtle blue," said Lou. "You are a real cowgirl Lou did you know that," said Hope. Jim sometimes calls me a cow bag (tongue in cheek)." Jim startled laughing and said, "Don't be a tiresome little cowgirl Louise."

Suddenly the phone rang. It was Jude and Lou went to speak to her after Hope was finished talking to her. Things were fine in Eugene and BJ had started her new job at the American Red Cross. Jim paid a visit to the toilet so he would be excused telephone duties. There was a picture of Martin Luther King in the hall. Someone who died before his time for merely trying to realize an earned and deserved dream. Well Jim had never had a dream that had come true yet. He was of the Stevie Wonder School of consciousness when it came to black America.

JACK NICHOLSON

They finished their cocktails and went through for dinner. It was sweet Virginia ham, mashed potato and sweet corn followed by fruit salad and yogurt. Lou's favoris/dessert. The tinned Ham was the best Jim had ever eaten in his life, it was remarkably good. And he had a second helping. With dinner they enjoyed a glass of Hock wine. Jim thought it wasn't the first time he had been in hock. After dinner they had Folgers Blue affricated coffee with demurer sugar, milk and cake, in the lounge.

Calum Cumming

CHAPTER TEN

They were on the road,it was eight in the morning and they were on the road to Mexico. They kept up with the pace of the freeway, 90MPH was de rigueur on the concrete grooved freeway of i5 as someone fish tailed in front of them going onto the fast lane where life was hotter and worth a vomit. The weather guy on the radio said the mercury was going to hit 80 F today.

Jim was driving and pretty soon they were in Anaheim, just passing through winter I say. Jim noticed the big wheel turning in a theme park. He said to Lou, "I used to work in the carnival in Aberdeen. It was my first job after leaving school I was a bingo caller. Two little ducks 22 unlucky for some 13. "Was it a serious job Jim? Why did you give it up?" said Lou interested. "The family that ran the carnival were the Coronas a ramifying but tight knit family of show business traveling people. The summer ended the job came to an end but it was a taste of show business. I always wanted to work on the waltzers as a spinner they were the cool guys." Replied Jim. Lou said, "But you are a traveling man Jim you are half Cairde Sinn Fein. For your mom is a Card, the top clan that laughs out at their little dung heap of dead fleas—Totally cool." Jim laughed and said, "I remember once on a building site a tinker gaffer of a drainage coy took out his glass eye in front of me and gave it a polish, he said it's a little

Irish today Jim." Lou started giggling uncontrollably and realized how much she loved James Dean Jr.

They drove on, drove on until they were eventually free of the strangulation of LA's Freeways. "Slow down a bit," Said Lou, "It's not a race you know." "I don't want to be driving in Mexico in the dark blame it on the sunshine don't blame it on the moonlight don't blame it on the good times don't blame it on the boogie." Said Jim. "Have it your way," said Lou. "But don't blame it on the American." And Jim honked the horn to indicate he understood and he slowed down to 70MPH.

They went past San Diego in a whirl it sat at the bottom of the bay the entire blue gray navy ships in the harbor. They saw a blue and white seven pointed Mares Truck. Their truck drivers were the safest in the USA thought Jim. Soon they were in the desert and the faces and bodies of native America seemed to be an intangible part of the landscape. Immutable and camouflaged like the rock and sand and cactus.

They slowed down to 55MPH for the car was beginning to burn up, the radiator was red hot and Jim didn't fancy blowing a gasket. They had bought some polish sausage, bread and Monterey Jack cheese from the Italian Deli. They stopped at a lay by and feasted. They had a large bottle of Evian still water with them. Lou had bought a couple of bananas trust her to think of their hot spot into Lou's mind. They stopped at a petrol station to get gas. It was part of the PEMEX state controlled oil industry. For Mexico was a democratic socialist republic with a president. Jim got out of the car and a man came and filled up the car with gas. It cost 100 pesos about $10, cheap. They then found the route for San Felipe by following the road signs to La Paz at the bottom of Baja. San Felipe was some 150 miles away and between them and their destination was nothing but dessert?

They were soon out of Mexicali and back on the road. It was 3PM and everything was slumbering in the mid afternoon sun. The road was as straight as a dye and went straight ahead until you could no longer see it in the shimmering heat of the horizon. Centerline and height control of the road followed a cambered gradient that was built on the flat sandy contour. There was no traffic on the road and they were alone with their car and no radio. The tarmac on the road seemed measly to Jim and you could make out the macadam of the sub base below the tar wearing coarse. There was so little traffic beyond the border town that the specification of the road did not need to be beefed up for it was adequate.

Every 5 miles or so was an icon at the eastern road verge of the Madonna and Child the baby Jesus. It was if it had been placed there by unseen eyes in the mountain ridge to the west of the road. Sometimes they would see clouds of dust thrown up by horses to the west, they were wild mustangs and Lou told Jim that she could ride a horse. The movie star Kurt Russell had taught her. Jim said, "Russell is a sept of the Cumming clan as indeed are the Nivens." Lou replied, "I always knew you were Hollywood royalty James." If only the Captain had gone to Hollywood thought Jim with sagacity. As it was he was smoking himself to death with one good lung in The Outer Hebrides in Scotland.

About 70 miles into their journey they came to a roadside bar with an overhead shuttered open window so they stopped for a beer. It was incongruous finding a tiny road bar in the middle of nowhere. The senorita was middle aged and she wore a fresh flower in her tied up straight shiny black hair. She said, "Buenos deas," Lou said "Dos Sol porvavor." They sat on the upright wooden log that faced the bar, paid for their drinks and drank Sol.

Everything was quiet, shipshape and Bristol fashion.

Lou said to Jim, "Do you think there will ever be world peace Jim?" Jim replied, "Yeah I think the world is desperate for peace once we get away from the attitude of the cynics who think they know everything but are so unelaborated it is beyond belief. Scotland is full of narrow-minded men who respect nothing except money and aggression. They never have a job and make me sick to the spleen." Those kind of people are afraid of change because it would involve individual change and they can't handle that sort of courage, that kind of long term professionalism." "Round and round the ragged rock the ragged rascal ran." Said Jim. "I follow you, Jim, in years alone." "I respect you wifely come let me bress thee in my arms." He held his wife tenderly and the Senorita smiled happily.

They finished their beers and drove the last leg into San Felipe. In a tic they could make out the ocean-The sea of Cortez. It was dusk when they arrived in San Felipe and the grasshoppers were noisily munching through the dark with a fluttering sound a sound like wings. They looked for a motel and found

JACK NICHOLSON

The Botany Motel in the dark. Trees swirled silently in the dark outside the car window as they stopped at the motel. Lou yearned for the day to be over for she was tired after the long sunny drive.

An old Mexican man with spectacles waited for them in the cramped room of check in. He spoke English for it was mainly Americans who stayed here and it was off-season. After check in Lou and Jim walked back to the car clutching the door key. They picked up the skyline bag and went into their room. Lou and Jim sat on the edge of the double bed. Except for this it was like any other motel bedroom with a clean bathroom and a TV. Jim held Lou's hand and warmed it in his own. He said, "Lou we came."

Jim lit a cigarette and put on the PAL TV. He found the movie channel, it was Internal Affairs with Richard Gere. He played a scavenging corrupt LA cop who was a disgrace to the uniform. It was a good movie with Gere at his best as the bent cop and love rat. They watched the last part of the movie. Gere enjoys being beaten up in the movie. His character is that of the misogynistic masochist.

Who dishes it out to women but can't take a beating himself.

"We're talking about women," Said Lou. "And you are my partner." An advert came on the PAL TV and made them both laugh. It was about women with an overactive bladder,Teena Lady. They both rejected old age until they were ready for it. But both Lou and Jim realized that childhood and old age was best. It was an instinctive loving thing.

The Movie was over and they were both filled with renewed confidence for neither of them were callow youth.

"You know that I will be the provider Jim when you are ready to write. "Ready to right Scotland," said Jim. "I am as rare as you jewel."

"Jim, tell me you love me"
"Deadpan best Fife-I love you Lou"
"You are such a quiet girl Lou, storing it all up inside like thermal bricks."
"You know I can be a handful like a Super star."
"You have such sensitive hands Lou."
"I'm knuckling European Jim as well as American Jim."
"For our beautiful child Lou."
"Any danger of a song Jim?"

Jim succumbed to her passion and kissed her on the double bed.

FOR I WILL GIVE YOU THE MORNING STAR

"In the sunset of an age and an epoch we may write that for epitaph of the men who were of it. They went quiet and brave from the lands they loved, though seldom of that rare love they might speak. It was not in them to tell in words of the earth that moved and lived and abided, their love and enduring life. And who knows at the last what memories of it were with them. The springs and the winters of this land and all the sounds and scents of it that had once been theirs, deep, and a passion of their blood and spirit, those four who died in France? With them we may say there died a thing older than themselves. These

were the last of the peasants, the last of the Old Scots folk". . .
"From Sunset Song," said Lisa and she started to cry softly in the old Mexican night.

They then undressed quietly and went to bed and slept; holding each other all night.

In the morning Lou rose early and said to Jim tenderly. "Will you call me Lisa now Jim for I have had a shining epiphany in the night-a moment of self realization and now I want you to call me Lisa for the rest of my life." "Whatever you say tootsie for I prefer Lisa to Elodeas for that place is very strange and not fully known to me. Lisa is short for Elizabeth, The god given child."

Lisa went and had a shower and felt renewed. Filled with renewed optimism, filled with renewed pride. She came through from the bathroom and put on her black Armani's and a clean white tee shirt. Jim was watching the news in bed and Lisa said I would go and get us some breakfast darling. Filled Tortillas, orange juice and coffee. Does that sound good? "Sure beats a kick in the head," said Goofy.

Lisa went into the sunshine and went to get them some breakfast. She walked past the sombreros on the lovely shoreline. She turned young and old heads alike keeping the Mexicans on their toes. She found the carry out store and went in. Two young girls were serving and Lisa said, "Buenos," to them. Lisa thought they must be twin sisters for they looked alike and were beautiful. They were dressed in traditional Mexican clothes of bright floral skirts and draw collar blouses. She ordered the food and drink by ostentation. She paid and left a tip for the lovely girls.

Jim was up and dressed when she got back and they ate their breakfast and drank the orange juice and coffee. The tortillas were good with refried beans and the refreshing bite of lime relish.

They then went out and explored the beach. On the beach were many rusted hulks of old sardine boats. Left stranded on the beach like immobile whales. Left to die like the elephants graveyard in Glasgow or the Orkney class salmon boats on Loch Steisevat in Leverburgh. It was not neglect for like Scotland it was a spiritual thing where the old replaced by the new was left to the fiefdom of nature by The Sea of Cortez. They walked around the derelict boats quietly and both understood this that it was not neglect but merely transformation and renewal. For the San Felipe men were good fishermen and also bible-read. For like the Jews and Arabs they would be content to allow Jesus to be a fisher of their souls.

They went down to the beach resort and sat on a concrete step above the sand. A little Mexican mongrel dog came up to them. In a tic she was all over Jim and licking him in the face. She wouldn't stop licking him in the face for she liked a man's lap to sit on. Jim said to Lisa, "What a lovely little dog." Lisa replied, "Give a dog a bone she adores you Jim." For Jim loved all animals and dogs and cats loved him. The little dog sat patiently at their feet and Jim cuddled her ears with his hand. He cleaned his face of microbial dog goober and felt the little scar that he had from the ingrown hair in Grant's house. It was inflamed and angry the wound had got infected. He thought nothing of it and said to Lisa, "It's a pity we couldn't take this "pink" little dog with us back to Oregon." A van drove past and hooted it's horn and then the little dog ran off back to its paradise in San Felipe. For she was a clever little dog and knew how to get food for herself. Lisa and Jim went down to the water edge and Jim washed his face in the brine. It was too cold to swim in for it was off-season and the water was cool.

They held hands and paddled in the sea of Cortez. They then went to the beachfront bar and had Tequila with a Sol Chaser. It was mescal and it had a big kick. Lisa said to Jim, "I want to put up the tent in the motel room this afternoon I have some Oregon mushroom do you want to do some with me?" "Nun," said Jim. "I'm too Jewish Lisa I don't like to lose self control you know that of me. I don't mind if you do some in the motel."

They walked back leisurely to the motel and Jim noticed the green water out the back of the motel it was raw sewage. The façade of the motel was exposed for him. An American in a Mexico plate Buick drove past them. It had a bullet hole in the windshield and the man was a gorilla. He looked like a gang boss who had emigrated from Pittsburgh.

The whole hippy vibe was a west coast thing. If they stayed here any longer Lisa reckoned it was going to rain. They went into their room and Jim said to Lisa, "Did you check out the show back there? That guy was a gangster and this motel is definitely third world." Lisa put up the tent in the little room; it was a pentangle and could probably sharpen razor blades.

Nutty Lisa took her mushroom and waited inside the tent. Waited to get high, waited to get the repetitive flash backs of a mild LSD trip. It was her 5th trip on LSD. Jim lay on the bed and switched the blue glare of the PAL TV on. He found a movie he liked. It was A Bridge Too Far with Sean Connery. All about the 1st Airborne parachute regiment and Anaheim. He swigged on his ice cold Sol.

Lisa had started tripping and was hearing string quartets in her ears. It was a piece in transition. She lit up a fag and used the omnipresent black ashtray. Jim said to her, "Try it in a minor," or that was what she thought he had said. She thought her legs were going to fall off. Meanwhile Jim watched Sean and the barking mad mental patients who have escaped into the wood in Holland. Sean said "Perhaps they know something we don't". . .

Jim felt like popping his wife. "But I don't think so," said Lisa from the pentangle. "It's going to rain," said Lisa solemnly. "A golden shower," said Jim going to use the bathroom. "I'm thinking of going to a commune," said Lisa "Open with similar motion close with piano phase," said Lisa. "A damned raccoon just ran up my leg," shouted Lisa. There are no raccoons in San Felipe.

Lisa was at the height of her short mild trip now and she wondered what new guy was coming over later. Jim came back to the bedroom and wondered if this place had fleas and rats, for where there was water borne sewage there was always rats. Lisa said, "I'm ready dear the doors open." Jim started laughing at her in the tent. He went and joined her as the war on the PAL TV droned on. She said, "Don't take away the music, everything else has gone, don't take away your loving." Jim said, "Wise up you silly little bitch."

"You may find yourself in a beautiful house with a beautiful wife and you may ask yourself let the days go by water flowing underground." Said Lisa. Jim replied, "Once in a lifetime-same as it ever was". . .
"Strike the pose Lisa get your panties off." Said Jim. And he took her in the tent roughly and fired in his muck.

Lisa was on her back after that.

"It's nearly supper time now," Said Jim from the double bed. Lisa had come down from her trip,she said she was off for a shower. She took all her clothes off and sat on the edge of the bed sulkily. They were like an old married couple. Jim bent towards her and gently kissed the nape of her neck for he knew she liked that. He said softly, "I love you sweetheart, I hope you won't go near LSD again." "It was a good trip Jim I loved when you broke me on, do you want me to suck your cock Jim?" No baby it is all right. I can smell your vagina on my fingers. There is nothing better than the fresh smell of vulva on your fingers after breakfast. Your vagina smells wonderful Lisa. You are so sexually attractive to me I love your vagina." Then he bent down and kissed his wife's vulva gently." A place where there are no men just the sky and the air and the animal inside of her human form.

Lisa went and got a shower and Jim smoked a cigarette and smelt his fingers while he watched the end of the movie. Sean Connery came back with only four fingers from his company,

They decided to go out at six to get supper at a restaurant. There was a Tacos Joint near them and everything was back to normal now. When they were walking along the boardwalk of a darkened building near the restaurant a young Mexican was sitting facing them in the growing darkness with his poncho and sombrero on. Jim could only make him out by his silhouette and the whites of his eyes. The young man suddenly said "Heh Gringo Une Cigarillo Pourvavore!" Jim Threw a smoke at him and Lisa started laughing in the Semi darkness at the gaucho. They went into the Restaurant and had beef Tacos and Tecate beer, the Supper was delicious and cheap as well. They were gone Back to the States the next day. Where there was plenty Rooms for both of them. Jim was left with the thought of A boat and he wished it were the season so they could Have gone for a midnight swim although now it was chill. The sea of Cortez contained killer whales and dolphins Lisa had told Jim and he was reminded of Moby Dick and Captain Ahab. He had seen the movie twice and read the baby Novella once. Herman Melville was a giant. The male Killer whale leaves the pod in order to get its aggression Piss out and Jim had realized long ago that he had left His family in order to be with his wife. He did not feel Aggression towards her though for like the Tao symbol there had become symmetry in their relationship and in Bed together they fitted perfectly like a circle for Lisa was his best friend. How is it possible to suddenly lose a real Female friend he discovered? For that is what had Happened with Jim and his last black girlfriend Elaine. It had ended like Mary Queen Of Scots gets her head Chopped off.

The thought chilled him for life was brief. It is impossible to lose a real friend he thought there was merely temporary easement. He really hoped that he would see Elaine again. At perhaps the end of his middle age. For it was Jim that had chopped Elaine's head off suddenly like a guillotine with virtually no warning. She had gone into hiding after Jim and Lisa had made the west end of Glasgow they.

They walked along the quiet beachfront and held hands. The night had come on suddenly. Jim said, "The next time we come to Mexico lets go to Mexico City and see the fly borne dung in the air like the elephants and Africa." "The vast colossus of humanity," replied Lisa.

They went back to the motel and took Grant's pent-angular tent down and Jim stowed it in the car. Ready for their trip back up the Baja California peninsula towards Mexicali.

They traveled back the next morning to the USA and the stress of modern technological life. The kinetics of it all. The goldfish bowl of Portland where they would be treated cheaply like a bottle of bleach.

Perhaps it is forest of Durries where the Scots pine grow,where the crows are always building their sties. I have a sty in my eye-so someone out there loves me-it's an old wife's tale but carries weight like the Queen carries her years, stoically. In amongst the human suffering-in amongst the lost human bundle of hopes, human fears and also suffering. The detritus of humanity where your surname is pinned to your door all there is to distinguish you from the mimetic of the parrot. YOU MUST ENDURE. To the very end of the long muddy road.

Carla said it was a lot of old fish when I tried to elicit some sort of human response from her after I had lost my head completely and spilled my guts out about my family. And yet the crows of Durries still build their sties never at rest for as the crow flies the mile is shortest. And complete no more no less than a complete mile straight as Running Wolf's iron head arrow.

The story ended in Portland one rainy night where Jim sick with streptococcus and high on penicillin and beer, (after visiting the the Belmont clinic for the poor for he did not have health insurance), arrived at the Blue Moon with Lisa. Jewel was waiting for them at the door with her Blue coat on she said, "Entrez sil vous plait" They went in and Jim dropped his gurning face,was he excited to see Jewel again. The entrance light was flashing seductively. And who was sitting at the bar if it was not THE MADONNA herself. She had made the trip,just this once for she was cats and eats dogs. A family creature the cusped LEO with her black Armani's on and her Italian Naples work wear boots. Like the ones Jim had until they tilted on a building site in Edinburgh. She said to Lisa, "Right that's it, oh dear oh dear". . .
For Lisa was the next big future star after THE MADONNA. It was just a question of time. Sitting with Madonna was Grant and Charles and Miguel keeping a drum on to the Euro beat. For Madonna was part Macleod part Mackenzie and fully the COMMON. Fingers delving into filth on the ground. She looked lovely and was wearing Chloe perfume. Desperate for a dance for this was a house night-Jack had seen to that and the MC was playing in the

corner. 5432 as we went warp factor two . . . Lisa had a Scotch and Jim had a bottle of Bud to keep his Streptococcus Company. Planet Spaceships, For THE MADONNA had made the trip from New York to Portland to wish Adele well on her trip home.

Jack had called her, "Ooh it's so god ooh it's so god," sang Madonna on the phone.

"It's been a long time Nona," said Jim. "This evening is sinister," said Nona and that's the way we like it for fear is the key . . . right Jim." "Feel the fear Nona for it takes courage to enjoy yourself." Said Lisa. For Lisa was the $million baby. No one fazed Lisa thought Jim. She would have belted Madonna. So there was a little jealousy in the air, that did not mean a catfight where the fluff would fly for Jim had always loved Madonna as a sister.

Jack walked in and right up to the bar. He ordered a JD and coke. The wake of him was groveling. For he left a trail of Romeo Y Juliet cigar smoke furrowing in through the open door. It was no night for strangers- it was any night to be twenty-one. Adele and Running Wolf were already seated around the mini buffet. The power of it all left Jim wishing he were Jack. Madonna kissed Jim quickly a stolen kiss in the darkness, and said, "I love you Jim." This was punctuated by the max of the disco entertainment. Lisa left things to ferment like shaken marbles. For it was Knuckle Nucleon cousin Jack.

Cousin Jack scotched his JD and then ordered another one. He wasn't like Jim Morrison, he was shaking his hips around the bar. Jack was showing chinks in his armor though,he had received a letter from Jacks Clarke that day and it was going to be the no no Camelot except Jack wasn't about to lose part of his cranium like orange leather melon skin.

The rain dogs the rain dogs thought Jack. There is a light that never goes out. Grant tried to strong arm Jack with conversation but he wasn't up for that. A strong wind blew in the night as the chiller system simultaneously kicked in behind the bar.

Carla had come up to the door and had tried to seek out the Oscar for it was time to settle the bad blood between them. Jack and Carla. Jack and Carla. The Jail is not my sun thought Carla. She was sailing solo and rabid and would have done a staffy solid crap on the floor. Madonna told a joke to try to crack the static in the air. She said, "What do you call a barrel imitating a fanny?" "I don't know?" said Jim; "A clitoris all sort," said Madonna. Everyone started laughing.

"Tonight right," said Lisa. For she wasn't about to take prisoners from either Madonna or that Midland tart Banes.

Somehow Carla found her way into the bar she must have slithered in through the keyhole like cigarette smoke-very clever but hardly worth the effort.

Billy Patterson was waiting outside.

Taking it to the streets. Jack spotted Carla out of the corner of his brown partially obscured disc. He made a run for the mini buffet and grabbed a raspberry cheesecake. He planted it right on her face. Running Wolf stood up and before he could say Come on

JACK NICHOLSON

Jack Carla was left on the floor like a little cheesy cake,for she were a Bad Enoch little bitch. It was a rash moment of madness from cousin Jack. Lisa stood up and said to Jim, "I'll give her a good licking." "Get the cream," replied Jim.

It was journey's end for Carla was not about to get up. Billy Patterson wasn't about to get his tea either for he had been barred entry by Jewel.

Hollywood stars only come together now and again.

It has been a hard day's night thought Jack and Jim.

Calum Cumming